ác

Regions of Tomorrow

Maurice Ash

Regions of Tomorrow

TOWARDS THE OPEN CITY

SCHOCKEN BOOKS · NEW YORK

to the Memory of Dorothy Elmhirst

Published in U.S.A. in 1969
by Schocken Books Inc.
67 Park Avenue
New York, N.Y. 10016
Copyright ©1969 Maurice A. Ash
Library of Congress Catalog Card No. 70-85676
Printed in Great Britain

contents

list of illustrations

'. . . and the sun, already down was manifest in the living tongue of fire darting towards the zenith, falling and darting again, ever more pale and languid, and doomed no sooner lit to be extinguished. This phenomenon, if I remember rightly, was characteristic of my region. Things are perhaps different today. Though I fail to see, never having left my region, what right I have to speak of its characteristics. No, I never escaped, and even the limits of my region were unknown to me. But I felt they were far away. But this feeling was based on nothing serious, it was a simple feeling. For if my region had ended no further than my feet could carry me, surely I would have felt it changing slowly. For regions do not suddenly end, as far as I know, but gradually merge into one another. And I never noticed anything of the kind, but however far I went, and in no matter what direction, it was always the same sky, always the same earth, precisely, day after day and night after night. On the other hand, if it is true that regions gradually merge into one another, and this remains to be proved, then I may well have left mine many times, thinking I was still within it. But I preferred to abide by my simple feeling and its voice that said, Molloy, your region is vast, you have never left it and you never shall.'

SAMUEL BECKETT: 'Molloy'

foreword

This book, although it makes demands upon its readers consistent with the philosophy by which our times are marked, is not for scholars; indeed, it risks being anti-academic. 'Research' lies close to the heart of a growing alienation between planning and ordinary people. This has happened because of a confusion about the nature of that truth which social research unearths. In particular, research into social forms which themselves have lost their meanings (because ordinary people have lost concern therewith) becomes classically 'academic'. This book, rather, speaks to all such in the now general community of the lettered—those busy with important affairs equally with those no matter how humbly engaged—as have a concern to translate into action our common grace of understanding.

Discussion held regularly over a number of years at the Town and Country Planning Association, together with the general discourse (both spoken and literary) of the planning fraternity, underlie what I have written—little of which is new. The only originality therein is perhaps comprised in the very demands I make—demands whereby I seek rigorously to charge with the debate those to whom it should belong: those who might act upon it and whose everyday actions, for better or for worse, will anyway determine it. Hence, with its hands clenched close to its chest, this book strains to break some of those bonds whereby, in Britain especially, an idealistic cast of thought—one that teaches us to despise as vulgar the everyday practicalities of life—has made of our ordinary good sense a hostage to inaction.

as the twig bends . . .

Town, village, hamlet, city—what these are we know, or suppose we do. We talk about them so often, make such free use of them, that anyway we don't need to know what they are. Their very use is what they are; they are words that have shown they serve us well enough to further our everyday miracle of communication, one with another.

They are, then, merely words? Surely, as words they must represent things in themselves more solid, tangible, somehow real?

What, though, if they should not? This, at the very least, is an interesting hypothesis. That is to say, that there might be no reality which the word 'town' merely serves to designate: but that the word 'town', perhaps by reason of its own usefulness, itself is the reality. So that, if the word is the reality, that which the word describes is not real; it is an idea, a form.

Actually, this is to weave no obscurantist web. At most, it reflects the mode of thought to which over the coming years, perhaps centuries, we shall probably accustom ourselves. It would indeed be no more than consistent with this mode if, amongst the social disciplines, what we call 'planning' were to lead the way in an emancipation from the structure of classical idealism that now rules our thoughts. For planning is about forms . . . the forms of habitation such as cities and towns, their articulation and development (this, alone, is what rationalises the detail of its practice); and, after all, the elucidation of forms is that vehicle left to the social disciplines by a philosophy arguing the inalienability of language from our understanding of those who use it. This is perhaps no more than to say that planning too must take note of the changing winds of ideas that are strongly sweeping across the world.

In any case, even if the foregoing can be taken no more than on trust, yet direct and practical consequences quickly flow from it: indeed, some most human consequences. To start with, our hypothesis about the relation between words and reality holds within it a renunciation of our immemorial search for the ideal town (or city, village, etc.). After all, this ideal is the supposed composite of a reality that perhaps is non-existent. The ideal city, your New Jerusalem, is a composite of all that seems good in cities, abstracted from all that seems bad, so that only what truly is of the city, of its essence, supposedly is left. This is a process made plausible, now one comes to think of it, only by the untenable notion that that from which thus we abstract, the city, is somehow real and not an idea. And yet your New Jerusalems! of how much of our present planning policies—our Severnsides and Humbersides—are they not the motivation? Surely the greater part! (Who amongst us has not harboured an ambition to see Brasilia builded here?) If such hopes are not quite doomed to dust, yet not surprisingly their materialisation ensues in the more than human problems of a Swindon.

This obsession with, this patterning of our thoughts upon, the ideal—for how much petty, intellectual tyranny, for how much blindness to the suffering of the humble, is it not responsible?—and for how much waste of argument? Would our official planning policies in Britain today, for instance, have become cast in terms of creating remote 'new cities'—huge projects, appealing to the eyes alike of certain kinds of architect and politician—would we have stomached these proposals, but for our idealisation of the city? For, to the hard and cruel costs of such projects, how little thought we have given! (Characteristically, we are now beginning to give such thought, but only after the policies that subsume these projects have begun to be implemented.) The costs here referred to are not just the cash costs of development, but the cost of opportunities thereby foregone, and the incalculable costs to be imposed upon those we must somehow persuade to populate these places. In comparison, however, with the frenetic possibility of building an ideal city, are costs like these such as to give our idealists pause?

The matter can only be presented thus, by way of derogatory questions, perhaps because nothing other than our subservience to idealism suggests itself to explain these aberrations of policy from common sense. How is it, then, that to oppose this one can even think in terms of the mere power of words? But then, words like 'town', 'village' or 'city' formulate certain ideas: these are the forms of human settlement—or some of them. As such, they do have a great power: in fact, the power of miracles, to make something of nothing. And this power does not derive from any ideal description of any of these forms. It comes from the every-day use of words—and from the marvel of their serviceability, each in a great complex of contexts.

This strange hypothesis, then, seems worth pursuing a little further. Maybe these sorts of words do have a validity of their own, an autonomy to be treated in its own right. Conversely, after all, no one has yet been able convincingly to ascribe objective criteria to, say, a 'town', nor to distinguish it by external stan-dards from a 'city', or a 'village'. When does the one become the other? And if they are (as some would have) a continuum, why do we need these different words at all? And why so often does one word, apparently satisfactorily translated from one language into another, describe a categorically different pheno-menon? Or the same language as used in different countries (Britain: America) do just the same thing?

In the realm with which we are here concerned—that of human settlements—some classifications have indeed been at-tempted from statistical data, such as to isolate the characteristics of specific categories of settlement, with a view to demonstrating their independent reality. For instance, logarithmic scales (for the *cognoscenti*) have been produced, showing that the patterns of traders performing sets of functions conform—albeit somewhat imperceptibly—to various categories of settlement. Since the categorisation of settlement in question is made upon the ascrip-tion of functions, the 'scientific' result is not altogether surprising. In other words, if you told an inhabitant that what he lived in was perforce a 'town', because functions x, y, z were performed there, he might bemusedly agree yet, one suspects, turn his back and just as likely start talking to his neighbour about the goings-on in their 'city' or 'village', as the situation might demand.

It is not good, of course, to scoff at scholarship. Most academic labour can be made to serve some purpose, even if often a different one from that intended by its authors. (Little need be lost, even of the often curious sociology of our times.) Yet it does seem unlikely that if what we call 'villages', 'towns', etc. exist as external realities, the sophisticated statistical analysis needed for their identification as such should simply confirm the presumably intuitive classifications of our ordinary speech. Yet alas! sociology has become notorious for its ponderous discoveries of the obvious. It is in fact strictly inconceivable that in our ordinary speech we should ever be dictated to by the academic pretensions of sociology to 'truth'. Our everyday words serve a quite different purpose. It would be incredible if they equally well served the complexities of a scientific unravelment of the natures of things—of things which, by definition, are supposed to exist independently of the language we have developed for that quite different purpose of communicating between ourselves.

Hence, we return to the surprisingly more plausible proposition: that there is indeed an autonomy to the words we use. It follows, that the purpose that these (more or less well) serve is that of their own clarification—or, to put it another way, of establishing their own currency: of being *au courant*. To say this, however, is not to imply that it must be sufficient in itself for us merely to communicate one with another—let alone, that such communication is all that, in turn, we might be competent to comment upon. It means, rather, in the first place, that such comment as we can make is necessarily constrained by the lack of authority of each one of us over language as our instrument: that we each indeed serve language, at least as much as it serves us, as also that none of us individually is possessed of final truth—that there is no such social truth. And this means, lastly, that our comment upon the matters from which language itself is inseparable—social matters—must be of the order of elucidation, rather than being diagnostic, aetiological; and, as such, it must treat of forms, rather than seek to discover laws of behaviour.

Yet, supposing a word like 'town' does become accepted in its own right as a valid communication between us, how is such a communication to be differentiated, selected, from all the other multitudinous human sounds by means of which we communicate? What order is there that distinguishes it from an abstract amalgam of other sounds like, at random, 'tree', 'mountain', 'house'—or whatever else? How is it distinguishable, if not by some objectively verifiable nature?—a nature that therefore obeys laws demonstrably independent of the language used to describe them—and, if not by this, by what other singular structure?

Presumably, by the structure of communication itself. When, for instance, we talk about a town, we do so in a certain structure of communication, of discourse. (Is all this, one wonders, to turn the world on its head? Maybe the world is ripe for turning.) We use the word 'town' in certain contexts, so perhaps it is these contexts which structure what a 'town' is. The situations we find ourselves in when we talk about a town are, indeed, the reality we seek. To use the word 'town', it may be, merely serves to order rather than to disorder our relationships. Upon such fragile and ever-shifting ground, then, upon an unending game we play together, is founded what we take to be real—and which indeed is real. Thus, the analysis of what a town is becomes the analysis of the structure of those situations in which in ordinary language we talk about towns.

How do we, in fact, talk about towns, or cities and villages? What structure does our discourse take about these forms? In the last analysis, such questions must be answered topologically: that is, in terms of space and time. (When we are treating of forms, this analysis is ultimately unavoidable—not least, of the forms of human settlement, where coming and going and staying and not going define so much the entities of which we speak.) Being forms, we talk about towns, cities and villages in terms of the spaces they occupy; and forms and space are indispensable each to our understanding of the other. What, therefore, we have to elucidate are the spatial ideas we associate with our discourse about these forms of human settlement.

Of course, we think (in our own, not the American, language) of a city as something big, in contrast to a town—and of a village as something small in contrast to a town. But we know that we cannot just apply exterior criteria of size in order to say that above such and such a size it is a city we are treating of, and, below it, a town. Indeed, we know that sometimes quite small settlements are considered to be cities, and large ones not. It is, therefore, to the spatial characteristics of size that we should perhaps first turn our attention. And, surely, a main characteristic deriving from the geometry of anything 'big' is the importance of whatever is internal to it in comparison with the relations between itself and what is external to it.

This seems very well to fit our common notion of a city. A city, big as it is, characteristically is preoccupied with its own affairs— has, indeed, this quality of 'self-sufficiency'—is inward-looking and, thus being corporate in kind, must be provided with definite boundaries against the world beyond. (Do we not still tend to associate a city with its walls?) In London to this day, for instance, the main exits leading to places outside it generally are insignificant, twisting streets (often, even, appallingly ill-signed) the logic of whose alignment really lies within the self-concerned complex of that city. And, furthermore, when what we otherwise would, because of its size, call a town, we rather call a city—as we do our cathedral cities, say, or the City of London—it is because of the weight of events within them, a weight that sharply separates them from the world beyond.

In spatial terms, then, it is in this sort of sense that we speak of a city. Yet this is not to infer that, because of this, such-and-such an agglomeration (New York, say) *is* a city, whilst another is not. We speak of any given agglomeration sometimes as a city sometimes as a town. It depends on the speaker's situation. We talk, for instance, of 'going to town', though when we have arrived there we may be in a city. When we think of a place corporately, politically, from afar (detachedly), or in a moment of pride, we may refer to it as a city; when we think of it in more intimate contexts, as close to us, or when moving about within it (going 'down-town'), it may rather be a town. Just because we give something a name—say, 'New York'—it does not make of it one of a class of things, immutably. The name is simply an invaluable cross-reference of discourse, a relationship between different situations. The spatial sense, then, in which the idea of a city resides in the manner just suggested, applies to such situations as call for use of the word 'city' if we are to understand one another and, therefore, if human situations are to exist at all.

Our idea of a town, and the spatial considerations that distinctly structure this form, similarly derive from the geometry of things that are relatively small. Inescapably, a town stands not alone but in relation to its surrounding region. Whereas that from which the city is separated is the 'countryside', the town, rather, relates to the country. In this sense, it partakes of a region. The market-town, to and from which like a pulse-beat the surrounding area goes, is archetypal in this respect. (In contrast, the pejorative phrase 'small-town mentality' conveys an imputation as to the falsity of any town's isolation or its would-be self-sufficiency.) It is true that we seem to make the distinction between 'town' and 'country'—rather, say, than between city and country. Indeed, Britain's system of local government, dating from the nineteenth century, is based on this distinction. And, of course, the expression 'dormitory town' is nowadays applied to a place that seems not to sustain its own daily life but rather to live upon its surrounding area. Yet town and country also is a conjunction—one, in fact, which signifies the field itself of planning; planning itself has had to develop not least in order to cope with the questionable boundaries we have created for ourselves. This conjunction—of 'town and country planning'—exemplifies that region which town and country inescapably compose by reason of the insufficiency of what we conceive as a town to live alone unto itself. This is why movement, or the possibility of movement, is so much associated with our idea of the town. Though it may even be New York or London to which we refer, we yet say that such and such a person has arrived 'in town'. And this notion of mobility has an association with things that are intimate, because it evokes a contrast with the wide spaces around the object of such mobility.

Now, although the pattern of our thoughts about these settlement forms may hopefully be somewhat as sketched above (and our thoughts are structured by patterns which cannot be arbitrary), yet it is more commonly supposed that our understanding about cities and towns depends upon our somehow knowing what each of these actually *is*. It is from this that our idealisations about urban form have developed. Yet the pitiful thing about a perhaps innate intellectual resistance to accepting an endless give and take of ever differing situations (such that no determination becomes possible about what the forms actually *are* around which those situations revolve), is that ultimately it merely cultivates stereotypes. (Basically, of course, it is for this same reason that slang is ever necessary to rescue language itself from decadence.) Meanings develop, after all, and forms are elucidated by their use in ever-changing contexts, and language in its intricacy and complexity allows our forms each to acknowledge a great variety. But when we try to fix an unchanging meaning to something, we also seek to fix the situation to which it relates. It is thus, by the making of immutable stereotypes, physically monumental, that we vainly hope to arrest that interference, so annoying to the idealist, which our social activities continuously create with our own understanding.

Thus architecture, and hence the aesthetics of architecture, have of recent years been playing a predominant part in British planning in its perplexed dealings with a changing situation, a situation otherwise incomprehensible to the well-educated idealists who govern us. Thus, also, we speak pejoratively of 'dormitory towns' because such towns destroy a stereotype and so our annoyance focusses upon them; we do not care to understand the changing contexts in which we speak of those towns. Rather, we are demonstrating our unwillingness to acknowledge the situation that has shaken to its roots our idealisation of the town. This, we do not want to know; the intelligentsia, for instance, have long since turned their backs upon the suburbs.

There nevertheless are times when some old word in all its articulation is not adequate to cope with a changing situation. This is when new forms are born, distinctions of a categoric nature—just as city and town remain separate forms, such that no amount of stretching or shrinking of one or the other can account for this difference. For some reason, new forms come most painfully to birth. They are preceded by lesions in communication between us, by a breaking in the cast of our thoughts, of a kind that eventually only new forms can treat. This, always, is the real revolution—in comparison, that is, with those physical revolutions that but pour new wine into old bottles. In our day and age, in which idealism exercises its tyrannies, any new settlement form must emerge past the obstacle of the already rotting remains (this does not refer to the tragic shells of a Venice or a Bath) of newly-made stereotypes, like those of the school of Corbusier. For we find ourselves alive at a moment when no sophisticated variation of the form of the city or the town can make for sensible communication about the world around us. Some new form of human settlement, it seems, is painfully being born.

Of course, new forms do not annihilate the old—though they may do so—and it is worth for a moment considering in the light of some further attempted topological analysis (that is, of its spatial character) whether one of the oldest and smallest of settlement forms, the village, might paradoxically not have a continuing role to play in this changing world. The village is of the country; it is thus inalienable from the space in which it lies, partaking of that space. This it manifests by the reverse process to the town's: the town is a focus of its region and, in varying rhythms, is visited by the surrounding inhabitants; whereas from a village (whether it be agricultural, mining or fishing) a generally diurnal flow emanates and gives significance to the surrounding area. Nor is it its 'smallness' that distinguishes the form of the village. (The village, in fact, in some sense paradoxically shares the character of isolation of the city.) We do not conceive of the village except as part of the space around it, more particularly of the fields that surround it. The village thus identifies a certain space—whereas the inward-looking city is so to speak abstracted from space. May it not be, therefore, that a new kind of village, the commuter village, could continue the perennial role of this ancient form in today's increasingly mobile life, a life of journeys daily being made?

B

At all events, it is in something after the foregoing manner that we must in general have arrived at our immemorial forms of human settlement . . . cities, villages, towns. Each as distinct forms, our minds have structured them—in a sense, mathematically. Of course, the foregoing ideas only scratch the surface. This is a surface, however, at which we all can scratch if we have a mind to do so. We are but uncovering ourselves. If we must cudgel our brains with philosophy to be allowed to do this, the exercise may nevertheless prove rewarding. If planning is about our neighbours, it should after all be possible for us each to understand it. And, until of late, we have supposed we did understand it: that we did know what a city was, or a town. The misunderstandings between us, however, are now proliferating. In our unending game of words, situations are developing around us in which, try as we may to keep pace with one another, meanings elude us; meantime, others amongst us, to try to preserve the meaning of 'city', make gigantic efforts to have the clock stand still. In compensation, however, other words in new combinations are struggling to establish their currency: 'spread city', 'urban region', 'metropolitan region', 'city-region'. There is a confusion here also, but it holds the hope of being a creative one, of moving towards a crystallisation of the idea of a region. For, with the mobilities now conferred upon us, it is regions we inhabit. Theirs is the form we are shaping by our discourse, to which thousands of tongues are contributing. And it is indeed our discourse that shapes this form. Regions are not simply there, awaiting our discovery of them; we make them, rather, by talking about them. For this is what it is to make civilisation. And it is because we strive after this that the form of the region is forcing itself upon us as a candidate for our consideration.

the accumulation of illusions

In Britain today, the fashion is for 'new cities'. It is to be hoped that this grandiosity will but mark the low-point of our decadence. Such a notion surely reflects an era when we have still supposed the cornucopia was full. Indeed, all too typically of an island people when it is no longer protected but merely insulated from realities by its position, romantic idealism now provides us with our readiest refuge. Somehow we have convinced ourselves that at this stage of the twentieth century the now archaic idea of the city has an even increased relevance to our problems. This conviction we officially are prepared to endorse to the tune of building, not just one, but numbers of New Jerusalems, as an integral part of our national planning policy.

It is facts all too concrete such as these that give urgency and validity to the abstract conjectures of the previous chapter. When policy verges upon the absurd, however, it is usually not because those who make it are unintelligent, or incompetent, but because they are perplexed. As we live by our ideas, so, when and if confusion spreads, our ideas will be the last things to change. When the only thing left to understand is that we are misunderstanding one another, then alone do we re-examine our ideas. Until that change finally occurs, the contradictions of policy will accumulate, to be ever more precariously, tendentiously, rationalised by those responsible for it.

Certainly, by merely looking on the ground at what is happening, one finds no credible pretext for our 'new cities' fantasy: nothing to justify so dramatic a reversal of everyday experience. One finds, for sure, what the pejorative term 'sprawl' has readily been invoked to describe. (It is a term too readily invoked, it seems, by your affronted intellectual idealist—from his point of detached advantage. Seen from near to, 'sprawl' is just a man and his wife establishing a home for their family.) One sees, that is, the countryside disappearing and yet not being replaced by anything one could recognise as the town or the city—but, surely, one does not observe any social distress accompanying this process itself. One sees, rather, a process of decongestion of our old cities—those cities wherein, historically, social distress has been associated precisely with their tight-packed human densities. (For sure, through the blind eye of our minds we still interpret this process as the spread of 'congestion'—thereby managing, miraculously, to combine in these twin developments the contradictory sins of sprawl and congestion.) One actually sees a spreading prosperity as the concomitant of the so-called 'exploding metropolis'. From the view point of the ordinarily involved participant of this process one does of course see certain disadvantages and certain affronts of each to each, of neighbour to neighbour, along with the manifest advantages; one might regard this, at one extreme, as the field, no more, in which our lives within certain tolerable limits must inevitably pass, or else as a merely wasteful disorder. What one does not overtly see in sprawl itself, however, is any sickening, inescapable social injustice, such as might call upon us to bring this whole process to an end and to bend our minds to some superhuman alternative—like the building of pristine and entire new cities quite elsewhere. Rather, then, it is in our mausoleum of ideas that an explanation of this extraordinary policy is to be found and that an independent process must have been unfolding.

Let us follow this process in sequence backwards towards its source. In Britain, then, it is now official policy to establish so-called 'counter-magnets' to the growth of the existing large agglomerations of population. These are to be the new cities. London, in particular, has been selected for this antidote (and the greater part of what here follows refers to this great prototype). This policy was developed—albeit in that hermetic, governmental atmosphere with which Britain is peculiarly cursed —to cope in its turn with developments for which a previous policy had inescapably shown itself inadequate. This previous policy was that of the Extended Green Belt—a policy which in its turn, naturally enough, had evolved from Green Belt policy itself. For sure, the Extended Green Belt (a kind of *reductio ad absurdum*) was an ephemeral thing, now never likely to be ratified. Yet it remains highly significant as a pointer to principles of thought.

In the mid-fifties, since the medicine of the Green Belt was clearly failing in its purpose, the official prescription (as is its way) was not for a change of medicine, but for more of the same. In this light, indeed, the 'new cities' idea itself was but a continuation of policy: that of at all costs pursuing the ephemera of urban 'self-containment'. (In this way, it may be noted, since to justify the resultant ever-increasing gap between settlements we have allowed ourselves to call this gap a 'region'—e.g. the South East—we have trapped ourselves into associating regionalism with an emptiness. To such ridiculous lengths can we be driven, unaware, by our preconceptions!) This strange policy of emptiness, and hence of the containment of urban entities, derived in its turn from that of establishing new towns around the old cities with a view to receiving such growth of population as these latter could no longer, were they to retain their recognisable form, contain. In its turn again, this 'new town' policy had evolved from the demonstration made in the earlier part of this century, of the economic and social practicability of planning and carrying through the construction of a town as such, and not merely as a fortuitous residue of other general activities. (Letchworth and Welwyn Garden City were, of course, the prototypes.) In its turn again, this demonstration had arisen out of the ideas of Ebenezer Howard, who had conceived a formula for conferring upon the ordinary individual the benefits which, separately, the city and the countryside potentially harbour, but which in the nineteenth century were each stifled by both industrial excess and rural stagnation. Ebenezer Howard, again, it can safely be claimed, was much influenced by the dichotomy of 'urban' and 'rural' which the Industrial Revolution had brought into relief, and which fascinated and obsessed the early sociologists and laid the foundations of their concern. We do not need to go back any further.

Now let us take the sequence forward again. This can be done

13

in the train not so much of principles as of the successive expediencies of policy. The Founding Fathers of sociology developed, it's true, various grandiose social cosmologies posited upon the key roles of urban and rural life. Howard was outwardly, however, more modest. Whilst he posited a schematic arrangement of settlements, such as might assimilate the contrary virtues of town and country, he was not concerned with what ostensibly exists—that is, the truth as revealed by some awesome system of thought—but with whatsoever in practice might become, might have the hope of practical realisation. Always practicable!— because always attuned to the kinds of lives people lived as he actually knew of them, not to the lives they would need to live in order to conform to a pattern pleasing to some grandiose system of order. Howard, to be sure, developed a schema—but it remained just a schema. That is, it had innumerable applications; it was not Utopian, because there was no rigidity about its relationships. If it was fixed upon anything at all, his schema was fixed upon the human personality—which itself cannot be fixed: upon the always unrealised potential of human beings for fulfilment.

Howard's ideas rapidly recruited support—significantly, not from academic social theorists so much as from practical men of vision. This support took the form of an experimental proof of some of the principles involved: a text-book exercise—Letchworth, and later Welwyn. Herein, however, danger lay. Experiments, being abstracted, are of their nature isolated. Socially (it is necessary to say) we indeed cannot experiment in the sense that this is physically possible; our social 'experiments' are carried out not from curiosity but from conviction. As such, they require an involvement of those concerned, such as in fact must destroy any more general reference. Social experiment, indeed, in so far as it has a valid sense at all, is a question of process: the state at which it arrives cannot be dissociated from, or like a physical experiment abstracted from, the state in which it began —nor that state in which it begins, from the past.

Perhaps those involved in the Letchworth and Welwyn projects were to a degree tricked by the climate of empirical thought. Howard's ideas seemed susceptible of 'proof', as might any theory of the physical universe. Not surprisingly, in this light, these projects acquired a quality of isolation all of their own and one, alas, that became integral in the mind of the public with the very principles of Howard's thought. The isolated new town thus seemed itself to represent what Ebenezer Howard stood for—and so 'garden city', as something apart from life, became a figure of fun and a term of mild contempt. Many of those relationships that were in fact crucial to Howard's schema came thereby to lie in discard. Even the first new towns attracted to themselves a minority precisely of those who, on one ground or another (the vegetarians, say, or the naturists) cherished and compounded the isolated quality of those enterprises. It was perhaps a genuine weakness of Howard's vision that he only in part deciphered the process of realising his vision—such that that part itself assumed a whole that was merely hypothetical. Or perhaps in his own times, no alternative was open to him. Yet this whole vision of Howard's, which was of clusters of towns related both to one another and to a common centre itself not appreciably greater than each separate town, at least disclaimed the notion of a town as something whose 'self-containment' could even be conceived.

The harm done by this misconception of the significance of those first new towns might not have been so serious had it not anyway coincided with a period in which confusion increasingly reigned over the credibility of certain ordinary terms. The suburb, for instance, was threatening our grasp of the meanings both of city and of countryside—and for so doing, of course, it has by the intelligentsia always been roundly abused. Sociologists also were claiming to discover 'villages' in cities. In this romantic climate, then, of salvaging something from the wreckage of the classical world, the thought of a new town's isolation as the urban epitome came ever more easily to mind—though, to those not so concerned with the classics, its credibility has never been plain.

So the next great phase of practical endeavour—the post-war building of 'satellite' new towns to take the 'overspill' of London —was launched under a cloud of conceptual confusion, a cloud at that time perhaps no bigger than a man's hand but certain to cover the sky. Their given status as 'satellites' was indicative of the principles underlying the foundation of these towns. They were to be paler imitations, lesser-scale replicas, of the primal city to which they owed their origins. In space they were to be isolated, 'self-contained', and, in so far as there were forces connecting them to the larger body these were, so to speak, umbilical attachments: attachments to be cut off when once the offspring was self-supporting. The Green Belt containing the primal city—and ensuring that it remained contained, as a city should be—was there as proof that the new towns, once established, were to take care of themselves. In this pattern of idealised relationships the roots of Ebenezer Howard's concern were already becoming unrecognisably overlaid.

Subscribers to Howard's vision have thus found themselves riding a tiger of ever larger dimensions. By the compromises of metaphor they have found themselves subscribing to mere appearances, appearances ever more remote from the substance of Howard's 'social city'. Certain architects and politicians, united by the superficial idealism of these times, have perverted the dynamics of Howard's thought. The age-old stereotypes have been called again in aid. For Howard, for instance, a new town had at most been but one of an inter-related cluster of towns: something moreover, in which expression would at least be awarded to each citizen of a civic democracy, individually to create his own home to his own taste. Nowadays, however, a new town is conceived as 'self-contained' yet subserving a city; vulnerable to the practice of architects to express their academic notions of urbanity, its development is legally consigned to a corporation quite autocratic in character, constructing houses for letting to tenants who have a negligible say in their design.

Now, social 'experiment' being a matter of process, the means used to bring about the great post-war surge of new town development in Britain are here relevant. To the government of the day, the significance of the new towns was conceived as a device for a massive public housing programme. The primary dialogue into which the government thus entered was with those in desperate need of public housing. It was such people who were supposedly willing, for the sake of decent shelter, totally to uproot themselves. This need of theirs, indeed, was what alone made the process practicable. All these considerations became embodied in the concept of 'overspill'—a harsh word for a harsh principle: it means, people so much in need of public housing that they will allow themselves to become the material manipulated by planners to fulfil an ideology. It is true, of course, that the suffering of pioneers has from time to time brought even great continents to life. Yet that third party to our historic dialogue—those dedicated to seeing Howard's vision realised—took a big risk in supporting the development of new towns upon such foundations as these. The process bridging the space between city and new town was quite at variance with the processes of Howard's own thought.

It was not to be long till the next stage in this sequence of events completed our conceptual confusions. The city has refused to remain contained, as a city properly should. It was, indeed, upon this containment that the fragile alliance of interests promoting the post-war policy of new towns was hinged. Without it, the common component of that policy—the apart but moderately-sized urban development—vanishes. Yet that little pin, the motor car, soon enough pricked through the city wall, and farewell . . . farewell a kingdom of illusions! As the isolated new town became ever more closely linked to its primal city, engulfed by the motorised tide, so, ironically, it became ever more prosperously conjoined to the national economy and attractive, not so much to those on the public housing lists as to those following their ordinary bents. In succeeding, the new town was thus defeating its latter-day sponsors' intentions. Human bigotry being what it is, however, we have rather preferred to stifle that success and discontinue the London new towns programme, in order to continue the pursuit of our original idealised purposes.

The bursting of the city's bounds has made the Green Belt—that keystone of policy, providing still the rationale which structures our planning practices—ever more anomalous. A well-intended yet revealing attempt by the government of the day, in the 1950s, to preserve the Green Belt's sanctity by doubling its width—the so-called Extended Green Belt—brought the absurdities of the situation to a head and so made inevitable the fabrication of a new strategy for planning. In due course, this strategy emerged precisely as an endorsement of the guiding principles of past policy. New cities replaced new towns. Larger and yet more remote developments were envisaged, as the necessary measure for preserving the precious principle of isolation and of that self-containment thought to epitomise 'urbanity'. As never before, this exercise became dependent upon 'overspill' for its implementation. In this process, the dialogue between the Government and all others concerned has been stretched to breaking-point. Planning and housing in particular have become ever less harmonised. Yet, so long as planning's voice is left to be uttered in official tones, it seems that at no matter what human cost the archaic forms of urban settlement are to be preserved.

The most immediate doubt about this 'new cities' policy focuses upon the surrounding confusion of the primal city. For, tacitly, the old city is no longer being contained: consequently, it must own to a region, and indeed planners are now generally prepared to recognise this. What they are debarred from doing, however, is even to treat of this new region, to consider it as an entity, because the only prescriptions in their medicine chest are devised for other conditions. In other words, planning has become impotent. Official policy thus depends on an inhibition upon realistic discourse. For to talk about the London metropolitan region (which now embraces the original new towns) as a 'city' no longer makes sense; it disrupts ordinary discourse. Yet, in the reigning official strategy of planning, there is no provision for that region's recognition. The latest strategy was cast in the old forms—yet here a new form is emerging.

Into our several metropolitan regions, growing multitudes of those simply willing to buy their own houses have come to live. There has been no official co-ordination of this movement with that of employment—nor of recreation, nor of any other positive initiation of policy. Planners themselves have become accustomed (dead-panned) to describing their part in the provision of this necessary residential space as 'unplanned planning'. Indeed, the only 'planned planning' in these regions—that of the new towns remaining to be completed—is being discontinued. And what of those persons who cannot afford to buy their way into these regions? Why, they are to be over-overspilt, to ever more remote distances! Only . . . only they are in fact resisting the ideology of planning. Increasingly desperate though the housing situation, the obsolescence, of the old conurbations is becoming, people are yet sluggish to uproot themselves to ever greater distances and away from that complex of opportunity we call the city-region. And the politicians, who are naturally sensitive to their constituents' feelings and, by comparison, care little for puristic planning, are responding by intensifying within the old cities the public provision of dwellings in ever less humane slabs of high flats. Thus, very neatly, planning endorses the most regressive of unplanned social developments, and is indeed preserving the form of the city—as a ghetto.

There is, to be sure, an ultimate restoration of logic in this replacement by policy of new towns by new cities. Perhaps, after all, we are coming full circle. For, unlike towns, cities as we know are by reason of their very size to be conceived as isolated entities. If 'self-containment' merely represents the urban ideal, the new city, not the new town, is the form we should always have been cultivating. Though logic, however, may here be restored, the doubt yet the more strongly adheres as to whether a dialogue concerning these old forms can any longer be carried on. Particularly is this so when it is accepted that in policy-making we have arrived at the idea of the 'new city' as a projection, still similar in kind, of the supposedly inadequate idea of the new town. In this respect, also, the direction being taken by policy is ever harder to reconcile with the ideas of Ebenezer Howard, no matter what genuflection towards these ideas it makes. In any case, however, the commitment of official policy to the form of the city at last corners it where its relevance to contemporary life can truly be examined. The very confusions attending the notion of the 'new city' help to throw some light upon this question of its relevance.

What, in fact, is supposed to be the relation of these new cities to their primal city? They are said to be 'counter-magnets' to the latter. Perhaps it is for this reason they are thought of as sharing a common region with the primal city; this region, after all, gives some sort of respectability to the relationships in question. (It was thus that the 'South East Region' was first so surprisingly introduced into discourse.) Whereas, then, the new towns were 'satellites', the new cities have become 'counter-magnets'. The latter metaphor emphasises a countervailing pull between equals. It also, however, admits the continuing tensions that must exist between such bodies; it accepts a connection between them, a compromise in their isolation. Hence, if such entities are each to preserve their identities, to be not sucked one into the other, it is reasonable to suppose that each must be large enough and distant enough from the other to make this possible. Thus, a 'region' can even be conceived of as a void, a necessary emptiness, between cities: a sort of social ether.

Yet there is a canker in this train of argument. To start with, a city in its newness most evidently is not the equal of a primal city. If in some significant sense, therefore, the one is to become the equal of the other, we must ask whether such a new city would not be greatly helped in this process of becoming equal by being located where it might benefit from those forces making for the agglomeration of the primal city; we must also therefore seriously ask whether the best location for its becoming an 'equal' might not differ from the best location for it to be and remain an 'equal'. In other words, we are back again to the question of process; likewise, incidentally, we are made ever more conscious, the more 'scientific' they become, of how dangerous it is to reason from analogies (such as 'satellite') with the physical universe. To use tools for empirical analysis of the natural world—the notion of 'critical urban mass' is an example, fashionably relevant—as if the conceptual analysis demanded by society must thereby be advanced, is at best pretentious.

In practice, if a new city is to be built up in competitive attraction to, and therefore distantly from, a primal city, this could certainly be done, but at a cost—a cost of some considerable order of greatness—indicated by those advantages of agglomeration foregone and to be compensated for. That a region, as such, however, might somehow secure that equality between these entities which would give significance to their relationship would no more make sense than does, say, the notion of such a 'regional' relationship between Manchester and Birmingham. Of course, these two cities do exert counter-attractions—stretching, perhaps, to the ends of the earth. But this does not make of the earth a region; nor does it take away the reality of our discourse about the separate regions of these two cities. In other words, following this line of supposition, your 'counter-magnet', be it but large and costly enough, might be located anywhere—anywhere, that is, where the government's writ runs. Between the notions of urban counter-magnets and of regions there is no connection.

Conversely, however, if a new city really is to partake of one region with its primal city, is to be built up through those self-same advantages, then whilst such a new city indeed might in-expensively and practically be achieved, yet it would not itself be a thing apart from and counter-magnetic to the other, but rather would complement the primal city's continuing growth. The plan for the Paris region, of course, accepts just such a logic, locating its large-scale new developments in relatively close proximity to old Paris, and (with ultimate logic) calling these not 'new cities' but, despite their considerable sizes (400,000), 'new towns'. In making even a bow to the realities of process, in other words, the idea of the 'new city' destroys itself.

Perhaps, in itself, there is no harm in the merely intellectual pursuit of the idea of the 'new city'. When, however, this idea comes to be interpreted by whosoever is responsible for imple-menting policy, the confusions are multiple. For instance, both those contradictory suppositions upon which the idea is based—that it does and does not share the regional potential of its primal city—have, in practice, separately been employed to justify major new urban developments: those respectively at Milton Keynes and Swindon. Livelihoods and human happiness for years to come are here at stake. As a result, what might have remained but harmless paper idealisations, have been transmuted into arbitrary, mandrinate processes. Government, in sanctioning these contradictions, becomes a law unto itself—and distasteful, surely, even to itself. It is not puppets, abstractions, which it finds itself shifting about—yet in human terms the justifications it must offer for its actions lack all consistency. What seems ideal must, as ever, be arbitrarily achieved. No wonder, then, that *The South East Study* of 1964 became a *de facto* official *plan* of action, yet did so without its ever in fact having made a study of the alternatives of action.

A genuine study of the alternatives now before land-use planning would be somewhat touched with anguish—because it would have to question, painfully, the forms by which we have lived and their continuing relevance. To ask the difficult questions—that is always the true criterion of 'study'. Merely to go on providing answers is to relapse into grandiosity—such grandiosity as new cities are made of. Yet if it is indeed painful to question anything from which our everyday activities readily flow (just as any questions we dare to ask of life itself are difficult and disturbing) so a failure to ask those questions may carry yet more painful consequences. In the present case, to continue unquestioningly to live by the idea of the city is at best to create in its name some huge one-class housing estate, basically constituted of the socially disestablished; simultaneously it is, as in London or any of our major cities, to abandon a place to the poor only—where a dwelling is expected to last two hundred and fifty years and where, because those poor are so reluctant to be 'over-spilt', the pressure is intense for ever higher, impersonal and expensive flats. From such 'cities', however, those rich enough to afford their own homes in reasonable spaces are in their millions escaping under the planners' averted eyes. Between 1951 and 1966 the population of London's outer metropolitan area grew by one and a half millions—from 3·5 to 5·0 million. Of this growth, only about 300,000 was able to occur in new towns. Abercrombie, upon whose calculations the strategy of London's planning was based, had posited a ratio of planned developments to normal accretion in the Outer Metropolitan Area precisely inverted—as of 5:1, instead of 1:5—to that actually achieved. The moral is not that new towns were failing in their purpose; individually, they were succeeding marvellously—though they were doing so because surprisingly they found themselves, not self-contained, but in an environment of growth. Rather, whilst the world was changing around them, planners were persisting over the creation of forms ever more meaningless. Only by mistake, indeed, do the London new towns stand out as a few examples of meaningful order in the resultant chaos of the emergent city-region.

Those who dare to perceive what is there, concretely on the ground, are now witnesses of the consequences of our being more concerned with the rectitude of our answers than with the asking of disturbing questions about our ideals. The make-believe world of planning, however, can no longer be left undisturbed.

the city lost

Sadly enough, the intellectuals' defence of that dying form, the city, is complicating the birth of its successor, the region. Indeed, there is danger that an impatient hurrying forward of that birth —in a perverted effort to bring the region to the aid of the city— will yet result in something hopelessly deformed. The 'South East Region', for instance, was a concept invented in Britain overnight to justify the development of new cities in what it was feared would otherwise have been a void. Till that moment, this concept of the South East had not entered into discourse, and in terms of social realities it still lacks all substance other than to sustain the private thoughts of certain official planners. Too readily, furthermore, in this as in other fields, one abuse leads to another and, regionalism having momentarily become a magic for our ills, upon deformed regions of physical planning we have had imposed on us by a well-meaning government equally dubious 'economic planning regions'. It will take regionalism a long time to recover from these ministrations.

It is true, of course, that there can be more than one kind of region, as also that the boundaries of different kinds of region might not coincide. A region, nevertheless, is not such just because a government, even with all the force it commands, says it is so. Yet governmental fiat is a powerful thing; it provides the parameters of many people's actions. If a government says regions shall exist, this becomes for a time a fact to be lived with. In the long run, however, if such entities do not serve the general dialogue about regions (if they are merely part of that government's monologue with itself) they will survive only if they perhaps serve some ulterior purpose: that is, if the government is using regionalism for some other purpose. There are reasons for thinking that both the 'economic planning regions' and the regions which physical planners, in order to create new cities,

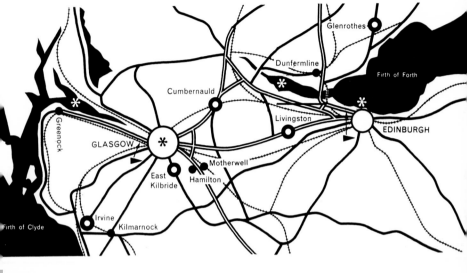

Motorways and Dual Carriageways completed by 1975
Other main routes
Railways
New Towns
Major Docks ▶ Airports

1. Central Scotland supplies a prime example of the realistic meaning of 'economic planning' in a regional context: namely, as concerned with the location of investment. Furthermore, it shows how investment in new towns can be the key to a regeneration of outworn industrial areas, supplying *foci* of growth and of new hopes within a depressed region. Arguably, Scotland's syndrome of industrial decline can be changed only by such an escape from the decay surrounding it.

Compiegne

Creil

Beauvais

Le Bourget

Pontoise

Mantes

Versailles

Trappes

Bry-sur-Marne
Noisy-le-Grand

Evry

Corbeil

Melun

Rambouillet

Vernon

Gaillon

Dreux

Louviers

Evreux

Elbeuf

Rouen

Lillebonne

Honfleur

Lisieux

Le Havre

Marne

Oise

Seine

Seine

Seine

Existing built-up area of Paris

Planned urbanisation

Leisure zones

Airports

Principal roads

Miles

Kilometres

0   10   20

0   10   20   30

have conjured up are on both the above-mentioned counts failing to advance an enduring dialogue about regionalism. The British government, dimly understanding that regionalism was a good (because, *ipso facto*, a coming) thing, has proceeded to use it as a vehicle to carry loads it was not designed to bear.

After all, what reality can there be in the idea of 'regional economic planning'? The planning of any economy, as nowadays understood, is a matter of regulating the flow of consumption and investment therein, mediated by its internal-external balance of payments. In this light a nation can have but one economy. A common but unique currency, after all, not only alone makes practicable the essential accounting of these matters, but also indicates the political parameters within which alone the notion of 'an economy' has meaning. No mere region of any country has an economy in this sense. Of course, however, regions might be characterised by some common economic feature—like, for instance, the industrial obsolescence of large areas of Britain. But these are not regions of 'economic planning'; they are regions which might be afforded special treatment by the national economy, perhaps by way of increased investment in them, but they cannot autonomously be planned because they themselves could not control or determine the in-flow and out-flow of funds. In fact, the suspicion already arises from this, that the purpose of 'economic planning regions' may not be for each such region to plan its economy—as the nation's economy should be planned,

---

2. The Paris plan of 1965 was a landmark of realism in the evolution of regionalism in Europe. 'Paris' was acknowledged to be henceforth a region: the city of the Seine Valley. The articulation of this region was proposed by inter-related 'new towns', each of the order of 400,000, the whole being organised in a broad corridor of development. One boundary of this corridor creates a shore-line, so to speak, to the noise nuisance of the new Paris Nord Airport. The use of land for leisure provides the positive setting in which the urban developments are placed. Arguably, only the French prefectural system of local administration, together with direct links with the Head of Government, will ensure the realisation of this Plan.

to maximise its growth—but rather to legitimise discrimination as between those regions in the allocation of investment. All political parties, after all, have debts to pay. Simply, they should be aware of what they traduce in the process.

This suspicion is enhanced by recognition of what that regional context really is—in Western, developed countries—that economic growth most self-evidently occurs within. This context is not that of 'economic planning regions', but of city-regions. Significantly, it was not upon these latter, nor any variation of them—although it was about these regions that the prior discourse had for several years been occuring—that the British government in 1965 conferred its authority. Yet city-regions are in one sense valid 'economic' regions. The location of investment within them is an issue crucial to their prosperity and social development. This, indeed, is the real sense in which, alone, 'regional economic planning' may endure. The government, however, invented other regions of its own and can be presumed to have done so for reasons other than those of economic growth. These reasons, clearly enough, were concerned, as has already been suggested, with something else; it was, in fact, something known as 'regional balance'.

The idea of regional balance has deep roots, deeper even than the mere discrimination of investment against one part of the country in favour of another. These roots lie in an idealistic view of the nature of the state. The notion here is that since regions exist, they must balance one another. This must happen because that is the nature of an ideal society. In this view, it is not what lies in the scales of balance that is important—not what the scales tell us about the properties of whatsoever they contain: it is the scales themselves. An ideal society is inherently in balance. If, therefore, regions must exist, they shall become organs of the state, partitions of it, because to tolerate them outside that structure would be disruptive. Each region, thus, must be a mini-state, an analogue of the state itself, such as to produce a balanced totality. In this way, the grandiose structure of 'economic planning regions' has served a certain purpose, as an attempt at building an ideal society. Whether such a structure is founded on sand can be left for time to tell. What matters in the present is that the structure, being in existence, has been made use of as a matter of convenience in just that way which fate holds harshly in store for all ideals. In this particular case, regionalism has degenerated into a disguise for special assistance upon a massive scale to the Development Areas where high unemployment has become indigenous. It is beside the point whether this policy itself is wise, or in the long-run humane. As regionalism, it holds the seeds of its own destruction because the 'balance' on which it is posited will not long be tolerated by those in fact disadvantaged by it.

The negative aspect of all this false, official regionalism lies in the harm it is doing to the understanding of those actual regions with which we surely shall be left when the present forced dialogue has been forgotten. For it is a main prop of the 'regional balance' thesis that the prosperous areas of the country—London and the Midlands—are 'congested'. Now this is one of the myths of our times. Its propagation depends upon our taking into our calculations not the urban regions characteristic of our own day and age but, rather, the crowded conurbations characteristic of the past. (This is one of the ways in which it is clearly demonstrated how backward-looking is the idealistic 'regional balance' thesis.) In the conurbation proper of London, the population density admittedly is of the order of 11,000 per square mile. That, to be sure, represents congestion. In the Greater London region, however, beyond the conurbation and up to between thirty and forty miles from the centre of London, say, the population density is something like 1,200 per square mile. These, surely, are categoric differences of order. Moreover, it is in the London metropolitan region that a phenomenal new growth is occurring and where a new urban form is developing—whilst the population of the conurbation proper is actually and continuously falling. In fact, the London metropolitan region is less congested than, say, Lancashire, or Staffordshire, or the West Riding. To foster the intuitive myth about the 'congestion' of our prosperous regions, to impute to these—whose prosperity in fact is closely related precisely to their growing dispersion and the resultant mobility—the characteristics of a form now defunct, is, alas, congenial to that natural alliance between the proponents of 'regional balance' and of the old ideology of physical planning. For the latter, in particular, it gives plausibility to the pursuit of grandiose ideas about 'new cities': remote, vast and veritable Brasilias, developed upon *tabulae rasae* in the still empty spaces of the land—your putative Humberside and Severnside new cities.

Really, these pristine new cities carry the stamp of political vanities. Being remote from realisation, they seem safe to boast about. Yet it is a reflection upon our climate of thought that these projects should have been proposed without exciting widespread derision. Our romantic fixation still upon the city is what would seem to account for this. Perhaps, after all, it is only natural that, as one witnesses the disintegration of something one cherishes, the more despairing should one's efforts become to retain it. By their very enormity, the conception of these new cities perhaps provides some reassurance that, as the past was, so shall the future be. Practically speaking, moreover, do we not by the end of this century somehow have to house so many millions more of our population? (With what gravity of statesmanship can such a question be asked and the statistics awesomely be deployed!) Hey presto, then, since to expand our present towns and cities would in truth be to destroy them, we shall provide new samples of the species, sprung to life armed cap-à-pie. The ancient forms must be preserved! This, after all, is all we have to guide us through the unintelligible difficulties of the times ahead. The alternative to this, for some, is hard to contemplate: that our forms themselves might change, not merely that destruction of the old might be entailed, but that we should have to grasp the significance of something new. To what lengths will we humans not go to avoid this!

Of course, great new cities, their towers cloud-capped, could be built by us. The cost, admittedly, might be enormous, the public expenditure inflationary, but these are merely matters of our priorities. The people, even, might somehow be persuaded to live in them—they will, after all, have to live somewhere. What gives pause to the idea, rather, is the very fact that we start from those cloud-capped towers; we start with the conclusion —and as for process, we relegate it along with the people concerned to insignificance. Yet the process is everything and, increasingly, there is cause to think it would end up quite differently than in cloud-capped towers, or even in cities at all.

We say to ourselves: 'In the year 2000 there will be another twenty million people in this country'—and, in a flash of instant planning, we have them all placed in great new cities. At some point, presumably, the old cities are to be stopped from growing. (Conveniently, this is a point that always seems distant and continually receding from practical action. Sometimes, this is known as having a strategy of action!) Then for twenty-five years or so, the new inhabitants will be required to live in some order of meanness, yet at least with their vision of those cloud-capped towers to sustain them. Or is it that the towers will be built first, slowly filling up as the generations pass? It is never quite made clear. What truly is clear, is that cities and all other forms of the human environment are but an indirect outcome of multitudes of autonomous activities, of relationships that functionally are self-regarding, so that if those activities cannot be practised (or only under handicap) a city if it grows at all will be only a poor deformed thing.

Anyone (A) in pursuit of his affairs and business, say with B, will have an impact upon X, Y and Z, who are not party to his affairs. That is what we understand as constituting the social environment and it is implicit in our notions of social space and of the very entities which, in occupying this, give this its meaning. The city is one such form of the human environment—one of those forms with which planning in particular is concerned. (Perhaps this helps to explain why planners need to know a little about nearly everything—why, inescapably, their own discipline is such a precarious amalgam of many others.) Such considerations as these are what underlie the dangers in our present talk about new cities. In so far as we see these entities, not as social environments but as artifacts, idealising their form, then the larger they are, the more tyrannous becomes the imposition upon those human beings we would have inhabit them of a given mode of life. Conceived as an architectural artifact, a new city becomes with a vengeance a machine for living in.

(In parenthesis, we should not find it altogether surprising that in capitalist countries the architecture of cities has a particular allure for Marxists—whether for Corbusier, for Niemeyer the architect of Brasilia, or for the architectural team of the Greater London Council. Marxism is a contemporary expression of idealist philosophy—and a highly romantic one, at that—and idealism's search for permanence inevitably finds an expression in monumentalist architecture. In the West, this impulse has on the whole been beneficially kept within bounds—though the romanticisation of proletariat culture has certainly made the change and humanisation of urban form more difficult. On balance, however, we in the West can be grateful for this deployment of architectural gifts. In the Communist world, on the contrary, it would appear that the absence of the abrasive forces of a liberal society has in architecture facilitated a stultifying monumentalism—or perhaps it is that the better minds there practise not architecture but politics? Marxism possibly works best in capitalist countries.)

Of its nature, the process by which some new city must evolve is different from that entailed in the building of a new town. A city is of its kind inward-looking, isolated, 'self-contained'. To construct such an entity from zero—an entity that is inherently big of its kind—is from the start to isolate it. Indeed were it rather to be built out of the relationships proffered by neighbouring settlements, its ultimate isolation would be fatally compromised: all that would then ensue would be a social sprawl, a wasteful perpetuation of needlessly extended social and economic linkages. To be sure, a new town can grow in just this way because its linkages with the primal city (and other new towns) are not extended and wasteful, but positively beneficial. But a remote new city must, from the moment of its conception, somehow have a powerful inward impulse of growth. In other words, it must be vastly capitalised.

The truth is, a city always is old. It is not enough just to conceive of a city for it to be achieved. The conceptual process that validates a city is one that cannot be hurried. It cannot be hurried because the complex of social and economic linkages that in our minds constitute a city cannot be forged overnight. If, in practical terms, we were to seek to overcome this difficulty by developing a 'new city' at quite abnormal speed, we could yet do so in practice only by cultivating for it an indiscriminate range of linkages with the world at large; and thereby we would effectively preclude, or long postpone, the attainment of a city-like identity. All too easily, in other words, the term 'new city' would become a euphemism for a merely large and nasty town.

This reasoning, though, does not apply to the notion of a new town, because a town precisely is identified as such through its links with the surrounding region. Thus, the factories in any one of London's new towns are not related functionally—only environmentally—to one another; rather, their manifold linkages are with businesses in other parts of that same London region. Because growth of this kind, then, is practicable and unexceptionable, the newness of a town is something of which we can conceive. The new town is located regionally; the new city, however, exists in an inconceivable void.

It is in any case incontestable that people everywhere are leaving the city. (The population of Greater London continues to fall—despite the frenzied provision of public housing within it—by some 90,000 per annum.) Hence, even the protagonists of new cities are coming to recognise that if ever one of their Brasilias were built, people would not be occupying it when it was finished. Somewhat desperately, therefore, the theory escapes to a yet more remote refuge. We must build, it says, not new cities as such but new city-regions, each apart in some distant locality. By this is meant a cluster of new settlements, in sum amounting to a city. (The strategy for developing the 'new city' of 250,000 inhabitants at Milton Keynes, for instance, after rejecting with much travail the 'linear city' concept, has opted for this solution of cluster development.) Now, this theory does outrage to the term 'city-region'. If Milton Keynes is a 'city-region', how shall we now discuss, say, the New York–Washington complex, or the London metropolitan area, for which the term was first brought into use? These are surely different things. ('Urban cluster' would perhaps suffice for your Milton Keyneses, if these must exist at all!) The truth is that to export the 'city-region' is not only as costly, messy and impracticable as to export the city: it is, furthermore, entirely pointless. The dispersed kind of environment to be achieved at a Milton Keynes could just as well be fashioned within the London metropolitan region, whilst yet benefiting from the social and economic linkages of involvement in that region—benefits such as must progressively be foregone the more remotely located from the city-region proper are your new urban clusters. How costly is the tyranny over our minds of old ideas!

The fact is that, in Britain as elsewhere today, the intellectual —himself an urban manifestation—is facing a dilemma. The city is the intellectual's natural pad; it is his hunting ground. In a very real sense, he has made the city in his image; the values of 'urbanity' are those conferred upon the city by the intellectual. (In much the same way, it is becoming recognised how the pronunciamenta of social science but reflect the type of people who become social scientists.) And now the city is disappearing; it is dissolving around the intellectual. To be sure, only in the last ten years has this come seriously to concern your 'urbanist'. Before that, he could with natural contempt continue to oppose a policy of building new towns as a solution to such problems as the city allowedly might own to. In these last ten years, however, with a finality that has had to be accepted, the city has burst its bounds. In so doing, it has washed the city planners with it out into open country—and there they have continued, trying still to re-make their artifacts and concocting ever-stranger avoidances of the facts. It is with astonishment that those others of us, who for so long have advocated new towns beyond our cities, now stare at this bid to take over these policies and to invert the values they represent. New towns designed by dispossessed urban intellectuals are anomalies we could readily dispense with.

Cumbernauld started it, and perhaps only in Scotland could it have happened. There, the overwhelming predominance of public over private house-building, combined with the abased rents that are part of the tragic syndrome of industrial decline, provide fertile ground for the well-meaning autocracy of officialdom. To make a semblance of a city, then, to epitomise 'urbanity', the houses at Cumbernauld were packed together twice as densely as in any other of Britain's (including Scotland's) new towns—which also means twice as densely as in any ordinary, historical town of comparable size in Britain. The effect was architectural, visual, external—and those for whom appearances are everything have applauded it across the world. The values embalmed in it, however, were supposedly 'urbanist' ones—those associated with people close-packed in their communal lives. Now no one need decry those values. The question is only as to their continuing relevance. It is deeply questionable, at a time when new horizons are being opened to the lives of ordinary people and when expanding opportunities are multiplying for them of at last realising their personal capabilities, as to whether it is right to confine them within romanticised stereotypes of the past. Those who have gone to live in Cumbernauld in desperate search of housing would have some reason for thinking that its environment was less adequate than all the publicity might have led them to suppose.

In fact, subsequently, the Cumbernauld principle has everywhere else fortunately been resisted. Whether it is because their nerve has failed them, or because real note has increasingly been taken of the kind of people we are, concrete responsibility has induced in those architect-planners charged with designing recent new towns solutions far more humanised than Cumbernauld itself. Yet the climate of thought remains clouded with sophisticated propositions: rather than to accept new towns as towns, to taste the disgrace of admitting after all that Ebenezer Howard was right, somehow to rediscover the city that is lost.

Two main sources have contributed to this murk. On the one hand, there have been those who would now realistically recognise the fact of humanity's motorisation, and so would allow for the use of the car within an urban environment by adapting our cities to certain specific standards of 'amenity'. On the other hand, there are those who would recognise the car only as the enemy it is of cities—no matter how much it may be the friend of man—and accordingly, at least in all new developments, would build only 'linear cities' wherein private motoring would if possible be barred and public motor-transport alone should be allowed, as suited to represent the communal values which the city after all (they think) exists to express. These veins of thought are in fact more complementary than contradictory to one another. They converge upon one uniform resolve: that the city as a form of life shall persist. Compared with this joint resolve— varying as principally it does only for the differing circumstances of existing cities and of cities to come—the equivocal role of private motoring in contemporary life seems unimportant. (Yet this is, in fact, an ambiguity fatal to the survival of the city.) Because these converging approaches to the problem promise, in the face of growing experience, the retention of those urban forms to which we are accustomed, they have commanded amongst Britain's Establishment a fashionable body of encouragement and approval.

The fashionably current 'environmental' approach to urban planning, then, should have this said about it: that it is physical rather than social in conception. The environment here in question is 'the built environment'; the conception is architectural and the standards that have been proposed are physical ones. Of course, these are real considerations. That we should be sensitive to and should savour our physical surroundings is one aspect of our being civilised at all—and is, therefore, in a sense social in kind. But an aesthetic evaluation of society, which is what is here at issue, is an altogether different matter. To be sure, the economic and social evaluation of any artist's work is all but irrelevant to its aesthetic worth (which is not as much as to say that it has no economic value). Also there is admittedly an environment of taste itself: a climate, so to speak, of creative physical activity. Yet society also has its environments—what we call 'markets', 'communities' and so forth—and our forms of urban settlement are amongst such social environments. We treat at our peril then, as for a period of years British policy at the highest level sought to do, of towns and cities as aesthetic artifacts. They are in fact but the indirect consequences of manifold social activities. Thus, to suggest that an 'environmental standard' for some city street should be set at such-and-such a through-traffic flow, is to risk setting up social tensions—there or elsewhere—which, in so far as they have not entered into the aesthetic determinants in question, could be dangerous and troublesome. Such troubles and dangers, being real, need to be estimated—and costed. This, however, is as much as to allow that, in this realm of human experience, whatsoever is physically aesthetic has some equally valid social evaluation upon it, quite independently. (Conversely, the artist can find a valid interest in a slum.) In practice, of course, and not surprisingly, the approach to urban form by way of 'the built environment' ends up in an architectural strait-jacket upon society, representing a stereotyped and socially unreal idea of contemporary life.

(At a yet deeper level of analysis, to make of the environment itself a function is a self-defeating process. Analogously, for instance, the climate of taste cannot be legislated or ordained. To change the environment, therefore, demands a practical knowledge of, and a respect for, those functions of whose indirect effects it is composed. That situation itself in which the idea of an environment makes for sensible discourse is, even though it concerns those circumstances common to all functional activities, necessarily as transient as are all other situations. Our makers of the environment can have but a limited say—a word from time to time—in everyday life; the same, after all, is true of, and precisely characteristic of, the landlord. And this is why planning cannot be Utopian; for Utopia is one unchanging situation, such that therein the environment has supposedly been usurped by some functionally determined regulatory process. The notion of the environment is thus a dangerous one of which to treat.)

As for the 'linear city' idea, what is most significant about it is its very name. That a single, immensely long strip of development can even claim to be called a 'city' is precisely because it is focused inwards upon its channel of public transportation. To retain this essentially inward-looking characteristic of the city, an overwhelming dependence upon one public mode of transport is logically called for. Indeed, even a modest allowance of private motoring leads in theory to a rapid and anomalous thickening of the housing line of your linear city, as also to a staggering multiplication of traffic lanes in the central channel. And, of course, to allow even such private mobility to anything so wayward as the ordinary human being could lead to deviations from the linear system such as the pattern could not admit. Why, such a human being might even cease accepting that he must look inwards: he might start seeking short cuts—looking outwards, in other words, to the establishment of activities just outside the 'city'. How disorderly it could become, then, if private motoring were allowed! Such, nevertheless, are the theoretical lengths to which certain apologists have been willing to go in their manipulation of human beings in order to preserve that form, the city, which effectively governs their cast of thought.

What is perhaps most sad about these intellectual strategems is that they form an alliance with poverty itself. They are predicated upon the poor and, if pressed about their relevance to contemporary life, it is often the poor they invoke. Those too poor to own a motor car, we are told, must be taken into account—and taken into account they are with a vengeance, to the point of determining the whole design of settlements. (This is the 'lowest common denominator' syndrome, with which we in Britain have become all too wearily familiar.) After all, perhaps, that there should be an alliance between the intellectual protagonists of proletariat culture and the 'urbanist' planners is not so extraordinary. Both are static in their attitudes to urban forms; both are idealistic and romantic in their thinking. Of course, that in the genuinely new forms of human settlement the poor have their essential part to play—this should go without saying. It is true, they might then not be any the less poor—but neither would the permanence of poverty have been made the pretext for making the world over in the antique mould. Perhaps, after all, it is a retribution special to Britain, that our conscience about the poor puts weights upon our ankles as we move into the changing world.

This, then, is the patchwork of confusions we presently endure through our vain attempt to bring the city back to life: regions that contradict themselves and cities that predicate their own destruction. These are the symptoms of some kind of convulsion. Even poverty itself, however, cannot excuse the poverty of our thought. The race now is for our ideas simply to catch up with our everyday experiences.

the person and planning

To be free: to be free: to be free. How insistently that need throbs inside us! (All of us? It doesn't matter: enough of us to make it real.) However, because this is the theme of the great political revolutions, with their flags bloodied, we discount its ordinary reality. Conventionally, in fact, we assume that freedom is from time to time 'won'—and then supposedly we have it and sit back to enjoy its fruits. It may not be so simple. It may be, for instance, that the values of freedom are largely negative ones: even, that to be free is to escape, and that of escaping there is no end. For, of the constraints that nature and the world place upon us there surely is no end. After one space, there is always another space, and yet another that will contain us. To be free, then, could in the last analysis be no more than to affirm that to be a person is real: to say, that the very idea of the person is valid— not as a social atom, part of the structure of an enclosing society, but as something autonomous.

Is it too far-fetched to pass from this, to saying, 'Look at the suburbs!'? Social idealists, devisers of great systems, have not liked to look at the suburbs; these do not conform to how things ought to be in a monumental order of things. Architecture, for instance, practically ignores their existence; for it, the suburbs simply should not be there. What are the suburbs, after all, but people engaged in a futile search for space? What more privacy, indeed, can significantly be enjoyed at ten-to-the-acre than at fifty? One may even be the more overlooked, the more exposed; and because in the suburbs there are fewer people to know about one's affairs, these affairs may in that gold-fish bowl be all the more closely known by one's neighbours. The crowded city, the argument goes, rather, is the place for personal anonymity, for the greatest exercise of choice, for everything, in fact, except space—and what is space but an emptiness?

Yet, are millions upon millions deluding themselves? (It is the measure of your intellectual's arrogance that he unquestionably thinks they are.) Of course, apologists seek to rationalise the matter in various ways. In particular, we say that for children the suburbs are so much better than the city; there, at least, space can be used for play! (On the other hand, Hyde Park never really does appear unduly crowded.) Perhaps in this there is a clue to the truth: that in the suburbs our children belong the more to us and the less to the city. They have a patch of our own garden to play in; we do not so easily lose them to their friends. In so far as our children, then, are but extensions of ourselves, all-important means of our self-identification, the space which the suburbs supply is simply an aid to our finding ourselves. Is this not, in fact, what the 'empty' space of the suburbs is for? It is a space in which we as persons the more exist, hence are the more 'free'. (Indeed, there is psychological evidence that our physical idea of ourselves expands as do the spaces enclosing us.) It is one step of freedom further removed from the all-demanding city— stifling, clamorous, importuning as this becomes to that self which each one of us, not without travail, generally manages to establish. By this, I do not mean to infer that those whom the city never stifles—the wealthy, say, or the intellectuals—are characteristically immature or unbalanced in their development (though, if the cap fits, it may as well be worn). I am thinking, rather, of the ordinarily mature person who, as life carves him out of the dead stone in which he lies, chipping the superfluities away, finds himself ever more alone: a person. To such as these, the little space the suburbs may offer is yet an affirmation of their own private existence. There do seem, after all, to be things about the ordinary human being which even the greatest theorists of social systems seem incapable of comprehending.

Of course, this is to speculate at the verges of the psychologist's territory, and even though the planner may need to understand a little about a lot, he must beware of such dabbling. In other words, it would not do now to attempt to construct a theory of the pattern of human settlements based upon a theory of the development of human personality. There is nowadays a temptation, it is true, to attempt something of this kind, because increasingly a cycle is appearing of movement to and from cities, suburbs and the like, coincident with age. (Together with the poor, the young seem to be inheriting the centre.) But the time for this attempt, if ever, is not yet, nor this the place. The fact of personal autonomy itself is all that now needs to be accepted. Such acceptance is, however, bound to focus attention upon the kind of people we are and to bring home to those who still would constrain us within the invisible walls of the city, that they are the gaolers of humanity.

Presumably, it could be claimed that humanity has long been imprisoning itself, and liking it. For centuries, after all, we have been pouring into the cities. But because of our love of cities? Because of cities as such, as a form of life to be followed for its own sake? Or, rather, because that was then men's road to freedom? If one prefers the latter premise—if one's predilection is to consider the energies of mankind, his endowment, rather than the products—one naturally goes on to ask which road those energies now are taking.

The direction this road till quite recently had taken was, for sure, that marked out by the 'office revolution'. Even more than the industrial revolution, which crowded the factories, the office revolution of the last hundred years but confirmed the city in its ancient role. The telephone, the carbon, the typewriter and a

---

3. Planning provides the otherwise non-existent connection between these two worlds. A new civilisation is being made in America's city-regions—admirable, enviable. Because the forces at work, however, are segregatory as between rich and poor (far more deeply so than between white and black) a dreadful price in social divisiveness is being paid for this civilisation. American planning suffers, incongruously, from a European sickness: urban romanticism. Thus, whilst the ghettos have been spreading at a frightening rate, planners as here in Philadelphia have been concentrating their efforts upon monumental architecture in decaying city centres as a talisman of urbanity. If the urban crisis is to be resolved, a positive social role will have to be awarded to planning.

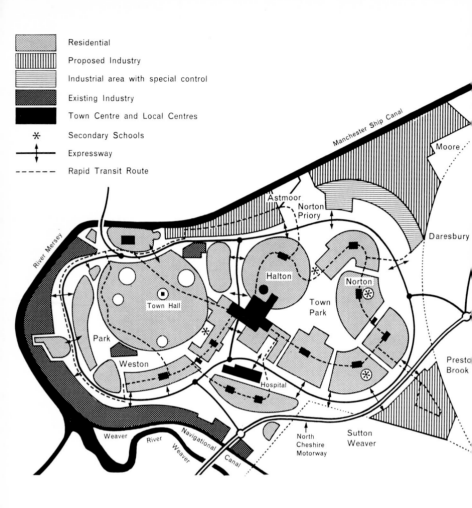

4. This is an example of latter-day (1966) pattern-making. The basic figure-of-eight is constituted of a public transport system. This makes for a variation of the 'linear city'; as such, it is inward-looking and rigidly self-contained, its *raison d'être* being the pursuit of an essential urbanity. It is easier, however, to make physical patterns when a captive, supine public is what supposedly one is catering for. Runcorn, nevertheless, is barely ten miles from Liverpool and it must be doubted whether, in the circumstances, architectural design could impose self-containment upon it. It is anyway questionable whether a new town is merely a lump of urbanity lifted out of a city. Car ownership in the London new towns, for instance, allows 61 % of households at least one car: in the conurbation itself, only 42 %. The days are over when urban form was dictated by the inarticulate masses.

variety of other, now simple-seeming tools of commerce, rivalled coal and iron in ruling the movements of great masses of men. Admittedly, as a result, the term 'conurbation' had to supplement our use of 'city' in discourse about these matters. The conurbation was simply the expanding city—yet still a form of the city, something differentiated and hence contained against the countryside by the uniformity of its bricks and mortar. Its mere expansion was certainly causing certain internal stresses and re-orderings of its structure. Industries were moving of their own volition to the peripheries, to escape those costs of congestion they themselves directly bore—even, in the case of London, moving as far out as Slough. The centres were becoming more simply commercial, whilst their ever-greater pull of employment reacted with the residential pull of the suburbs to produce that peculiar daily heart-beat we associate with the notion of the conurbation as a variation of the form of a city. Still, however, the form remained intact. People could escape, for sure, but only to the suburbs where the city went with them and embraced them still.

The conurbation has been anchored to the city by the 'external economies' of commerce. The great majority of offices, for instance, are not owned by their occupiers, but rented. Such a provision of readily available accommodation is of crucial importance to commercial enterprise, with all its risks, its tenuous connections, and its multiplicity of small trading organisations; it is an 'external economy' essential to it. The centre is the inevitable place to find this pool of accommodation. Personal communication, likewise, has been the immemorial accompaniment of commerce; the 'opportunity costs' of communicating by other means are inordinate. (An office building, misjudged by even a few hundred yards in London, can still cost the speculative developer a fortune.) Naturally, then, it is in the centre that business gathers and which itself is defined by the 'external economies' of commerce there available. Nevertheless, for all the weight of this anchor to the conurbation, the structure is breaking up.

Man, who made the city, is unmaking it. That what he made he has hallowed, is irrelevant. That he does these seemingly

D

fickle things is because of what lies in himself—and has always lain there. He is taking a new road because he is being offered new opportunities of freedom. These opportunities, it must be said, are not just technological in origin. Their background is also economic in the most general sense: in the management of economies to ensure 'full employment'—that is, in such a way that jobs if anything are looking for people, rather than people for jobs. There is, of course, no certitude about this as a continuing state of affairs (about what else is there, anyway?). An economy can yet have great structural faults, which only cataclysmic action might correct; and the world economy is still far from under rational management. But there now is much certainty concerning the factors in these equations and, this being so, those with their hands on the levers of control are above all inhibited from ever again using fear as one of their weapons. (If they did so, there would soon be others at the levers of control.) The fact, then, that if a person quits his job he no longer need fear he may never find another (one speaks in general terms) must have a profound effect upon what was formerly his resignation to remain where alone he might reasonably expect to find such another. Rather, he can now range more widely—and range, if he be a humble person, as widely perhaps as in former times the privilege of professional qualification allowed others to do—to take not only what work suits him, but where it suits him. And where it suits, rather than what it is, seems, in the nature of what we still insist upon calling 'work', to matter ever more and more. This is, then, an emancipation revolutionary in human history. One wonders if Keynes foresaw its effects upon the forms of human settlements.

Yet without the conferment by the motor car of personal mobility upon the ordinary person, it is doubtful if a mere extension of the suburbs would have been transformed, as indeed it has been, into the city-region. The motor car has conferred a radically new command of space upon people. The discussion is open as to whether the motor car has merely engineered mankind's retreat from the city. Arguably, for instance, people have never wanted all that opportunity the city supposedly offered;

material ambition, as the driving force, has perhaps been something of a myth, necessity having rather been the motivation—there are, after all, age-old predications of this. The motor car, on this hypothesis, has simply allowed of a withdrawal from importunities—or, at least, a maintenance at some acceptable level of a sort of balance between opportunity and a taking of life as it comes. This discussion itself hangs in balance. What merely illuminates it is the fact of the motor car's abetment to escape: to escape to a different space, such that one influences rather than is influenced by events, that one selects rather than is chosen by opportunity, and that one is the less assailed.

The car replaces courage in a man. It allows him to take journeys he would never have contemplated before. As we now know, the commuter tide of public transport into central London has halted and even turned, whilst between the edge of the conurbation and beyond it into the metropolitan region, a huge criss-cross pattern of private journeys is building up. Years ahead of London, in Detroit and other American city-regions, the outward flow of commuters now equals the inward flow. (In Los Angeles, again, the distinctions themselves are now meaningless.) Applied, thus, at the fulcrum of full-employment, the lever of the motor car is restructuring our forms of settlement. We are observing the ordinary man determined to have his cake and eat it—as aristocratic man, for centuries, has managed to do. There is an implacable force behind it.

It is, then, the ordinary person in command of mobility and opportunity—a phenomenon new on earth—that is the shaping force of our new forms. The home is no longer at risk with the job. Predictably and inexorably, therefore, jobs are being drawn towards the homes. Neither the industrial revolution, nor the office revolution, are any longer the shaping force of these events. Emancipated man himself is in control, and, for all their external economies, the centres of industry and commerce are disintegrating under this pressure and reforming themselves elsewhere. The jobs are moving to the suburbs, and beyond, at the behest of those who can command their presence there—albeit disadvantaging those who cannot so easily relocate themselves. In this sort of flux, great opportunities must surely lie for the re-shaping of all things.

What sort of man is it, then, who is thus making new space for himself? At least the sociological facts about him are becoming better understood, yet still bear reiteration. For one thing, he is coming to take leisure more seriously—an irony which the changing character of 'leisure' itself may go some way towards extenuating. (Leisure and work may in times to come become increasingly less distinguishable. The fetishistic character of work, as the totem of Western values, also seems bound to undergo change. 'Education' is likely to change its meaning along with these other changes.) People are not only marrying younger but setting up home independently of their parents much sooner. The idea of the family, under the impact of this trend, is thus being transformed. The proletarian culture of extended kinship is being put under a great strain. The idea of 'the home' is predominant and is becoming a space dedicated to a new sort of self-containment, made possible by an ever more sophisticated range of hardware, from television sets to deep-freezes, garbage disposers, etc., and fortified by private swimming-pools and (in America, at least) the 'rumpus' room, deemed indispensable to every new middle-class house. Adolescents, in their turn, are carving out space for themselves in the form of an autonomous teenage culture. Shopping habits are changing as those who supply the goods adapt their products to the new people we are, to allow of at most a once-weekly journey to the shops. People are more and more owning the houses they live in and thus are able to dictate the kind of houses that shall be built—and to be able thus to dictate is in itself to make more of one's own kind of space around oneself, more 'room' to be oneself.

To reiterate such salient points as these is not to assert—as often is done—that we are all becoming more 'middle-class'. This may not be so. It may rather be the case, as some experience already seems to show, that lower-income housing in the suburbs and beyond does not automatically impose a middle-class ethos upon the occupants. Working-class culture may well adapt itself, yet remain separate and still retain its hold in these circumstances. We cannot all be technocrats. Even in a mobile world, indeed, the poor will always be less mobile and less able to command space. Yet in their own way they too will certainly seek to command mobility and increasingly go to further their own interests wheresoever the money is good. To idealise the poor may thus become a little harder in future, for those who might still wish to do so. They too will want their private spaces and will not so docilely agree to inhabit the New Jerusalems provided by Corbusiers of the future. Whether these spaces should be segregated into ghettos of the poor is more to the point of planning.

The emancipation we are witnessing, whatever its fuller description might require, is producing one self-evident effect. The great dichotomy between 'rural' and 'urban' is breaking down—and, with it, all the grandiose systems of ideas that have depended thereupon. This is not to say that to speak still of 'town' and 'country' is futile. These terms, after all, have also merely physical references, relating on the one hand to human artifacts and on the other to Nature. Such distinctions may, in practice, still be useful; country parks, for instance, appertain as much as does agricultural land to Nature, and are in this sense distinct from towns. But what is absurd is to suppose that people still can be divided into townsmen and countrymen. This is the social distinction in the matter, and upon it no sensible settlement pattern could now be planned. Socially, the distinction is not worth making; we are becoming so homogenised by a culture which is neither urban nor rural that it calls for a new form of settlement to be articulated.

This, then, is a topsy-turvy world, yet what abides in it is a faith in the ordinary person. It is a faith one, alas, associates only with the more modest type of social reformer, such a one as Ebenezer Howard. The ordinary person, indeed, retains a surprising capacity to upturn even the most monumental of social designs. If respect for this capacity is what imbues modesty in a reformer, such a one's notions would seem more worth following through than those of the great system-makers. Certainly, if we do not understand the meaning of 'a person' we are disqualified from discussing what is happening to the environments we inhabit.

the dissolution of hierarchy

We are told that there is a hierarchy governing human settlements: that to understand this hierarchy is to realise why settlements are to be found where they are: they stand in their varying orders in strict relation one to another. This theory of human geography is the basis of that discipline's aspiration to the status of a science; it is something that can ostensibly be tested by observation, and as such it purports to demonstrate the operation of laws independent of the observers. This being so, it bars the path to any contrary hypothesis—as that our understanding of human settlements must simply be through elucidation of the forms that are anyway the product of our own discourse: that it is more fruitful to talk about such simple things as villages and cities, than about 'orders of settlement' and the hierarchical relationships between these.

The question at issue here is not whether the theory of settlement hierarchies is the right theory, but whether any such extrinsic theory of settlement relationships could anyway be valid. Now, to deprive a discipline of its 'scientific' status is not a deed to be contemplated lightly, in this day and age, when everyone supposes that to not rank as a scientist is to not be heeded: when to 'test' something is to do anything but put to the extraordinary test, by understanding one another reasonably well, that language in which we every moment discourse together. Some geographers, after all, have been at serious pains to try to identify the constituents of various hierarchies, and this theory does seem to make for at least some consistency of discussion amongst those who subscribe to it. All such discussion, amongst scholars who pursue it, is of course not obscurantist—gratifying though it may be to any of us, from time to time, to partake of the esoteric. Yet, in describing a place as being of such and such an order in a hierarchy, a geographer refers to something which

in ordinary speech and by us ordinary people will be quite otherwise conceived. To carry credibility, therefore—to be himself not
isolated by a jargon, rather than succeeding in isolating that
entity of which he seeks to establish the independent reality—
the geographer must demonstrate the practical significance of his
description, in particular the impact of 'hierarchies' upon the
layman in such a way that to the latter a translation of terms will
prove enlightening. So far, this demonstration has not been made.

It is not enough for the scientific geographer to describe things
as they are—despite the connotation of 'reality' that this might
seem to convey. To succeed, he must also prove that things could
not be other than they are. Merely to say what things are would
be to leave such a geographer open to the accusation that his
description of reality is adapted to his choice of terms. For instance, he must not be open to the allegation, not just that there
is no hierarchy of settlements, but that the orders of the hierarchy
are anything but immutable. There must be no arbitrary defini-
tions of such orders, each perhaps selected to suit the convenience
of some particular circumstance. Rather, the distinctions must be
verifiable, immanent and independent of situations. However,
should such definitive distinctions of settlement indeed exist, it
were perhaps a little strange that till now we have somehow got
by with such characteristically interchangeable terms as 'village',
'town' and 'city'—strange, but admittedly not impossible. Ordinary language assimilates only slowly the (always) necessary
technicalities of those with new insights. Yet, that to ordinary
speech the settlements in their hierarchy remain foreign, virtually unserviceable, casts suspicion upon the idea of hierarchical
distinctions itself. To say that at precisely such and such a point
a settlement becomes of one order rather than another will, indeed, carry little weight with anyone involved in relevant
affairs—a retailer, say, pondering whether to establish himself in
the place—because it will at best appear a statement merely of
how things presently are. To another retailer, or to the same
retailer in a different capacity (say, as the parent of school-
children), or to countless people in different situations, a different
order in a different hierarchy might make sense. Indeed, should

ever such a statement about hieratic order come to sway a practical decision—as, analogously, what he understands of the 'law' of supply and demand may perhaps sway a trader's decision about the price he asks for his goods—it would only do so because the very notion of 'hierarchy' had achieved a certain acceptance, in such wise that your retailer (say) found it helpful thus to explain his actions. The 'rule' in question would then merely be that which confirmed the currency of 'hierarchy'.

In other words, the condemnation of the theory of settlement hierarchies is not so much that it is false science, as that it is poor conceptualisation. A main reason for its lack of conviction is that as settlements become larger they clearly contain within themselves units comparable to those of a lesser 'order' than themselves. Towns acknowledge 'neighbourhoods', and cities have districts, and each of these in a rough and ready way perform those 'functions' whereby geographers have sought to identify the very orders of the hierarchy. Now, it is of the character of a hierarchy that its orders are distinct one from another; they do not contain one another—and certainly they could not partly contain and partly not contain one another—but rather they stand apart and are related only by the rigid forces of that hierarchy which alone holds them all in thrall. The plausibility, and therefore the conceptual usefulness, of the theory of settlement hierarchies breaks down particularly at this point. The things that a town (or a city) contains and the ways these inter-relate are precisely what makes a town a town and not simply another order of a hierarchy—say, a settlement of the third, fourth or fifth, etc., 'order'. Indeed, the internal and external relationships of a village, of a town or of a city are what are characteristic of each of those forms, and are precisely not of a hierarchical uniformity.

Does it all matter? Can the academic world not be left to its private devices? If it does matter, it is only because of the scientism, the false association of reality with quantification, which presently so bewitches us—and it is to the academic world, alas, that we look for our discoveries of scientific truth. False science results in poor conceptualisation, and poor conceptualisation impoverishes us all. It would, nevertheless, be unfair (and unkind) cavalierly to dismiss all the endeavour that has gone into the investigation of hierarchical relationships of settlements. Poor as this conceptualisation may be, yet in New Towns and on reclaimed lands (in Holland, for instance) these investigations have provided useful rules of thumb for practical decisions. What alone is deplorable about the pretensions of any false science is that they block the path to change. In describing things as presumptively they are, a false science inhibits the development of new concepts, new forms. It imposes Authority upon life.

It must be said, indeed, that the alliance between pseudoscience and the hierarchical theory of settlements is quite peculiarly tyrannical. To the would-be social scientist in his isolation as the keeper of social truth—a new-style priest, not communicant with general mankind—is here allied a notion that itself is, innately, autocratic. Further, this alliance is naturally congenial to your contemporary intellectual, whose habitat is precisely in the urban scene and who would much like to believe he exists at the centre of truth and authority. Altogether, it has combined to make a formidable body of opinion about the order to be imposed upon the world, about how errant, therefore, are those disorderly mortals, whose wayward activities increasingly are disturbing the proper pattern of our settlements. And, most directly, it is the emphasis which the theory of hierarchies is of its nature bound to put upon 'centres' which subordinates the way ordinary mortals might wish to live to that pattern, which urbanistic idealism (for that, ultimately, is what the hierarchic theory of settlements is) would impose upon us.

Centres are where those functions are carried out whereby the various orders of the hierarchy of settlements are distinguished and identified. There, in the centres, are made manifest the characteristic activities of each order. The centres not only serve to identify the orders of the hierarchy, they express in their varying importances the values of the hierarchy. The centre thus acquires an emotive significance somewhat analogous to that, in another sphere, of 'the heart'; it epitomises whatever order it is to which it relates and it stands for what essentially this is, its idealisation. Naturally, those who live and work in the centre—the rich, the clever, the males—consider themselves the purveyors of civilisation itself; and the bigger the centre, the more civilised supposedly are those who operate there. Civilisation itself, ultimately, is urbanity! Such, indeed, are the veins of thought implicit in the theory of hierarchies, strains all too conducive to such persons as actually exercise power in these matters—persons themselves denizens of the capital, of the centre of centres—to connive at every effort to retain those antique forms of settlement which best serve to perpetuate the general illusion of 'the centre'.

Yet the emphasis placed upon the centre has a still deeper purpose than that of describing the functions performed there. After all, 'centre' is in practice an imprecise concept; it is rare, and in most discussion not necessary, precisely to define the boundaries of a centre. (This is not to question that, in a general way, the activities carried on in the so-called 'centre' of any settlement may indeed bear some relationship to the latter's size.) The notion of a centre is important, rather, in so far as the whole entity in question would otherwise be difficult precisely to identify. Since precise identification of the order of any settlement is vital to the theory of hierarchies, a concentration of attention upon the centres of settlements becomes inescapable. The centre, therefore, by conferring identity upon what otherwise might physically and empirically be indeterminate—might, in fact, run the appalling risk of lacking scientific identity—becomes the cynosure of analytic interest. This, then, is an association of ideas that forcibly detracts from the importance of the everyday, the simple and the humble in human life, and exaggerates monumentality and the architectural appearances of cities, conferring upon these a quite spurious reality.

It is probably the emphasis upon the centre as that which identifies the whole which, above all, has made traditional thought in planning so deeply resistant to our changing society. For it is indeed the centre, its very integrity, that is threatened by our new settlement pattern. The out-of-town shopping centre, for instance, is anathema still to your British planner. Reactionary authority, under its usual disguise of municipal idealism, has gone to great lengths—as in the Haylock Park case—to inhibit these developments. Clearly, moreover, this particular phenomenon brings with it the collapse of the whole hieratic structure. (It is an attendant irony of this situation—not entirely fortuitous —that so many of our British town centres now supposedly ripe for redevelopment should, over the years, have come largely into the ownership of the public local authorities concerned. That Authority should yet again have guessed wrongly about life, however, is surely no ground for denying to the community as a whole the economic benefits of the kind of development it, with an increasing obviousness, wants to bring about.) Of course, manufacturing activities, in so far as these have been bearing their own costs of congestion, have long since abandoned the centres of settlements. Nowadays, however, this process is accelerating and many other activities are removing themselves from old centres, and yet doing so often without creating new ones, without, that is, creating complexes of functions that have any particular constitution, or that relate uniquely to any area of settlement.

We are thus experiencing the breakdown of credibility in the notion of centrality. The factory in green fields, the detached office complex (Croydon), the out-of-town shopping centre— these and other such phenomena are undermining the age-old association of a settlement with its centre. As with literature today, the plot is dissolving; as with painting, the process is superceding the product; so with our settlements, we must bring ourselves to acknowledge that the form has become fluid. If ever there was much usefulness in the notion of an area of settlement related, as it were heroically, to the range of functions performed at its centre, the idea is rapidly losing validity. In so far as one can still even entertain the notion of a settlement itself, this notion increasingly has a purely residential connotation. That those who live in 'a settlement' are tied even to whatsoever other functions may be situated there, is increasingly implausible; such persons may, for instance, shop for all or some commodities in a neighbouring area, and their neighbours in theirs. More likely, each area will in time share a 'shopping centre' that belongs to neither, but rather to itself because it relates to no other functions making thereby a centre of anything else. The ubiquity of the motor car is setting at naught the locational pulls of the static past. Such centres as now are coming into existence are, increasingly, functional not locational ones—shopping, commercial, educational, industrial centres, such as carry no implications of being set within any necessary kind of settlement, nor of life as a whole around them. They are not sub-centres of some greater centre of a settlement; rather, they are autonomous in character—and even they, sometimes, are far from being to any significant extent centres of their own particular functions.

We do not like these facts; they disturb our familiar ways. We try to retain our civic centres, because that is how to preserve our forms. That is why Coventry, for instance, of whose centre we are all so publicly proud, really is just the last spasm of the Middle Ages. (How much better would it not have been to have developed a few out-of-town shopping centres to serve that city!) Again, this is why the planning machinery is now swamped with redevelopment schemes for town centres that, in total, amount to economic nonsense. And again, in a simple way, one can see the same forces at work in the countryside, in areas of rural depopulation. An increasingly common formula for these areas is what sometimes is known as a 'key settlement' policy. This policy assumes that since rural population is declining, it were better to concentrate it in a relatively few of the existing settlements—villages or market towns—in order that at least a few good specimens of these forms should survive to give country people a congenial framework for their lives. The countryside, however, with the aid of the motor vehicle, has for decades past been regionalising itself. The school may be in one village, the church in another, the policeman in another, the district nurse in another. There is no centrality there any more, nor is this often essential to the maintenance of the fabric of the villages; indeed, development may continue in some or all of these as part of the process of replacing capital consumed (as quite normally this will be) at a rate greater than that of depopulation. In this particular situation, we can very clearly see how a policy posited on preserving the traditional forms of things—those forms in the light of which our planning decisions take their rationale—can, in the most practical way, stunt new forms of life that are struggling to emerge.

It would be best to admit to ourselves, then, that we are enduring the destruction of much by which we have lived—in this, as in what other fields not else? And the dissolution of old forms is certainly not automatically synonymous with the making of new ones. ('Chaos', however, might yet be a meaningful word, even when this alone gave order to our experience.) Yet not even this can excuse that romantic veneer behind which now we are all too frequently offered a refuge—the making of new cities, or the illusions of urbanity such as would re-create the centres of our old cities, peopled by architectural imaginations with shadows having no substance in contemporary ways of life. The truly clamant demand, rather, is for new forms, for hopeful expressions of a new discovery of reality. We are constrained by our human condition, indeed, not to re-cover in a dress of impossible reality the skeletons of history, but rather to discover a new reality and clothe it again with civilisation.

social science, form and planning

When old forms of our life decline—of course, it is sad. They have contained something of mankind's aspirations, have been a vehicle of civilisation. Of course it is sad, then, that cities are things of the past—not least, one suspects, because it leaves us naked to face the future. But, though sad, it is not wrong that these things happen—unless the very idea of what is wrong is to be associated with whatsoever is new (in which case, there is nothing we should not have to reformulate!). Change, in fact, need not occur only through degeneration, but through the vital action of new opportunities creating situations that demand new understandings between people.

Thus, if ideas of what is good or bad are to be applied at all (as inescapably they are) it must be to the particular examples of each and every form. We can, legitimately if crudely, think of a 'good' town; and this, and numerous other such adjectives, help confer upon all our forms their necessary variety, as they also explain how we ineluctably are bound to invest these forms with civilised qualities.

Obviously, then, there might be developed a consensus of criteria whereby the qualities of our various forms could be assessed. Moreover, these criteria could be quantified. In effect, for example, this is what we are doing when we are talking about urban 'densities' of various kinds—and there are all sorts of other yardsticks besides, such as we apply to our land-use planning problems. Never for a moment, however, does such quantification measure any kind of autonomous truth—though sometimes it seems supposed to be so doing. Quantification, indeed, is not reserved for the establishment of empirical law. Were I, for instance, to say that the public park is 'untidy' because the grass in it has been allowed to grow too long, and if I propose that six inches represents what is 'too long', my use of such quantification is neither right nor wrong; it is merely more or less serviceable, useful as elucidation, in the circumstances. Hence, the idea of form (the form of a 'park') does not exclude quantification as an aid to its articulation; but the idea of quantification, if thought of as the means of supplying a 'correct' answer, is not congenial with the idea of form.

To those who believe that human affairs must yield to scientific truth, as has the natural universe, this subordinate role of quantification to form is unacceptable ('subordinate' only in so far as, conversely, without quantification the natural sciences could not even be practised). The spell over us of quantification is such as to foster the widespread belief that society indeed holds its own truth, whose discovery must follow from the quantitative assessment of all possible social issues. To those who seek this truth, then, two courses are open. The course of idealism is one: of positing the ideal form and quantifying its dimensions. As has earlier been said, however, this is a perversion of the idea of form itself. Alternatively, your social quantifier overtly can entirely ignore all distinctions of form and, instead, seek some social measure, the very universality of which might command the truth about society as a whole—such a measure, then, as would itself supply the unifying order of what otherwise must become a meaningless conglomeration of activities. Thus, because values are what permeate—or seem to do so—all social action, and because money is the measure of value, monetary quantification has now become the ruling passion of those who would hold in their hands the key to social truth.

'Cost-benefit analysis' has lately emerged into public view as the tool of those who, ostensibly to replace the 'hunches' of an older class of ruler or administrator, wish to establish policies that demonstrably are true. Cost-benefit analysis aims at evaluating all the factors relevant to any given transaction but not directly expressed by that transaction itself. To evaluate all our social actions by cost-benefit analysis would, the extreme theory goes, and assuming the calculations were rightly made, provide us with accurate guides to each and every decision we had to take (and, incidentally, would do so without reference to the forms to which those decisions might apply). Investment decisions, say, in port complexes, the location of great airports, education, road expenditures, parks—all such things, which may or may not be expected themselves directly to yield a quantifiable return (yet which certainly must shape much of the life around them), could but their 'real' values be determined by cost-benefit analyses, would have decisions taken about them with an unclouded certainty. Their 'real' values would, of course, amongst other things embrace the costs they would require others to incur, both in the way of further investments and in the way of deprivations of existing investments—and so on, presumably, *ad infinitum*. Could but these calculations be made—the argument goes (and hitherto it is only their complexity that has prevented this being done)—we should truly have a science that superannuated all the vagueness inseparable from our incorrigible trafficking in work-a-day forms. To talk, say, about 'modernising' a city, or making a town more 'agreeable', etc., and judge any given investment in that light, would then become meaningless. Towns, after all, are not things we hitherto have much defined by their profitability, or even their wealth.

There's the rub! If indeed the values of so many things are, so to say, submerged it is surely because in the deepest sense they

---

5. Whether or not the plan proposed in 1967 by the Regional Economic Planning Council of the South East is ever implemented is unimportant compared with the fact that here, at last, there was recognition that London is a region. The Council perforce accepted the distant, disconnected 'new cities' given by official policy but, by specifying the planning of corridors of development to link those 'new cities' with the conurbation and hence with each other, it tacitly accepted the unity of the whole: the region of London. Whether, this step being taken, any relevance can still be ascribed to the 'new cities', remains to be seen. The plan is notable on two further counts. First, its evident lack of physical pattern-making signals the (welcome) arrival of social considerations into British planning. Second, the production of a regional plan for London had to wait upon a Council on which sat no professional planners engaged in statutory planning.

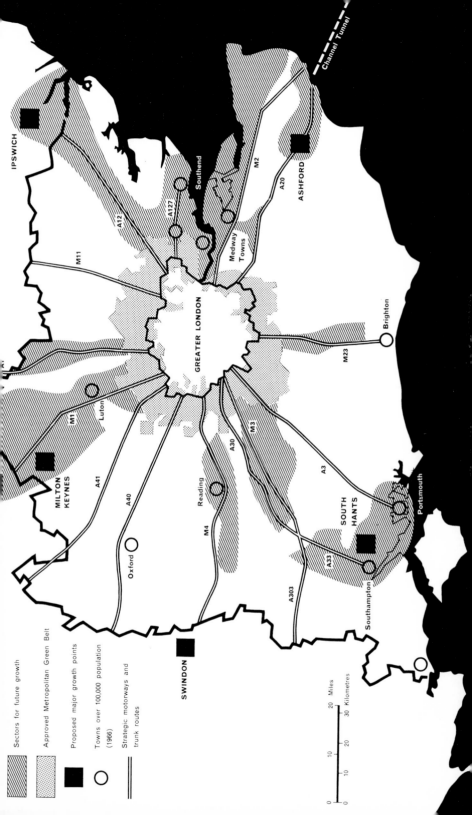

Sectors for future growth

Approved Metropolitan Green Belt

Proposed major growth points

Towns over 100,000 population (1966)

Strategic motorways and trunk routes

IPSWICH

Channel Tunnel

Southend

ASHFORD

A12

A127

M2

A20

M11

Medway Towns

GREATER LONDON

Brighton

M23

Luton

M1

M3

MILTON KEYNES

A41

A40

A30

A3

Reading

SOUTH HANTS

Oxford

M4

Portsmouth

A33

A303

Southampton

SWINDON

0   10   20   30 Kilometres
0   10   20 Miles

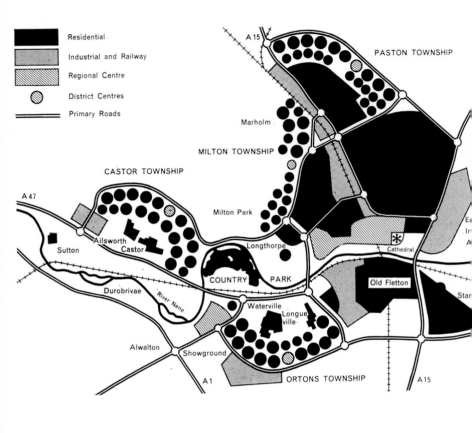

Residential

Industrial and Railway

Regional Centre

District Centres

Primary Roads

A 15

PASTON TOWNSHIP

Marholm

MILTON TOWNSHIP

CASTOR TOWNSHIP

A 47

Milton Park

Ailsworth

Castor

Longthorpe

Sutton

Cathedral

Ea
Ir
A

Durobrivae

River Nene

COUNTRY   PARK

Old Fletton

Star

Waterville

Longue
ville

Alwalton

Showground

A 1

ORTONS TOWNSHIP

A 15

6. Tom Hancock's plan for a 'new city' at Peterborough to take over-spill from London, 70 miles distant, is a sensitive expression of the possibilities of a contemporary urban environment. The residential densities, the sizes and relationships of the urban units, the phasing of development, the provision for leisure, the proposed social structure— all show the marks of a humane and realistic mind. It would be tragic if such a plan were not carried out. Yet is Peterborough in a meaningful relationship with London?

are out of currency: they are out of discourse and hence of significant relationship. Monetary measurement of value appertains merely to the situation, actual or potential, of priced exchange. What reason, then, is there to think that it is other than a function of that situation? a form of discourse therein, losing all significance when taken out of that situation? Economics, as an academic science, precisely holds that 'value' is measured at its margin—by prices agreed upon at the margins whereby each body of exchange is defined—yet economics is admittedly haunted by those 'values' not measured at the margin. Many economists recognise that there is, within their discipline's analytic framework, no option but to rest content with their 'marginal' rule of thumb; but some have wanted both to have their cake and eat it—and cost-benefit analysis has developed as a consequence.

Cost-benefit analysis would apply that measure which has been abstracted at the margin of economic activity and apply it generally to the body of that activity, even though it is only an abstraction therefrom which has given that measure its validity. Now a measure is part of the language of those who would apply it to something apart from their communication between themselves. If the use of a measure is limited to a certain situation, however, if it is not applicable unequivocally to that which it measures, then such a limitation must be one which governs its linguistic role, its part in the process of communication. Given this limitation in its use, to contend none the less that, by means of an arbitary modification (in which those who use it have not participated) it applies where in fact it is not used is, without proof, to presume the existence of an external reality about which we cannot communicate; in other words, it is to practise mysticism. The ultimate irony about cost-benefit analysis, of course, is that it is a mysticism practised in order itself to contend that a science of society, one that can prove what is and is not socially true, exists.

The fact is, it is an assumption much to be questioned that either price or cost measure 'value'. Value is indeed pervasive of society and in some significant, topological sense defines social

E

boundaries. This may well be true. But that, being measurable, it must therefore be something externally real, or that measurement as such any more establishes the independent reality of value than it does that of, say, 'height' or 'width'—this is quite another matter. A simple, if radical, alternative could be simply that a price just is—a price. It is an aid to discourse, a part of language capable of nuance, subject to qualification and of changing interpretation, yet of proven serviceability in human affairs. As such, the monetary measure is relevant to those situations in which those who use it to communicate with one another thereby find they order their affairs. To extend its use obscurely beyond any such situation, however, is like (say) trying to discuss a problem in physics with an economist. It is a temptation for unscrupulousness: in non-academic terms—bullshit.

Nevertheless, our anxiety for certainty, the debased rationalism of our culture, is such that many who are not economists would seize upon those measurabilities which that study seems to offer, in order to turn the process of measurement into truth itself—so that whatsoever can be measured must be true, and everything must submit to a common measure. When, however, not what it measures but the measure itself becomes what's real, it is time for any 'science' to reveal the idealism it is actually disguising, what form the social 'truth' takes that it predicates.

It may seem extraordinary that a digression (such as the foregoing is) into economic principles should be necessary in a work upon the forms of human settlements. If this is so, it is only because these two disciplines have hitherto trod their separate paths. Has the concept of the Green Belt ever been subjected to the scrutiny of economists? It has to do with urban forms—and forms have been beyond the province of economics. Has, conversely, the investment return upon say, an underground railway system, or a container dock complex, been related to its role in the developing patterns of settlements? How would you financially quantify such patterns of development? Is it, then, too large a claim to make, that on the one hand an obsession with social stereotypes—of town, city, village and countryside—and on the other hand the pursuit of a non-existent social truth, have horribly combined to limit our mental horizons? If so, the hope-lessness of replacing the old processes of 'hunch' by a still more misleading scientism—a process of false certainties—becomes readily understandable. The real alternative to each of these courses, surely, is the development of new forms, in terms of which our ordinary judgement can as ever be exercised.

Where cost-benefit analysis and urban form confront each other is indeed a meeting-point at which social science comes face to face with itself. It is a meeting that cannot be postponed much longer. From the devious alleys and burrows down which it has run, social science will have to come out into the light of day. Our civilisation cannot stand much more damage from this source—all such damage as ensues (perhaps in particular to education) from a mechanistic attitude to society. Social science will openly have to declare whether it proposes to reveal truths about our society as immutable as those we have about the working of the natural world—or, if not, what alternative and more modest role might belong to it. Pending this moment, how-ever, the rest of us must get along as best we can with under-standing the world we live in.

In this everyday world, there occurs a commonplace distinction between activities that pay for themselves and those that are subsidised. The bias of an attitude which supposes that financial measurement reveals social truth, is to contend that the subsid-ised activities are of a lower order than the paying ones—and that those subsidised activities should be made to pay. Such an attitude overlooks, as it is bound to do, the possibility that the activities that pay may do so because of those activities that are subsidised. Indirect effects of that sort are an inconvenience to measurement, such that a policy of their elimination is sometimes advocated by means of the application of stricter accounting to the loss-making activities. Thus, for instance, the requirement has been laid down that London Airport (Heathrow) should 'pay' —although very few airports the world over strictly pay for themselves, or ever would have been constructed had that principle been applied. (As, initially, municipal airports they have been part of the changing pattern of municipal form.) Again, the transport systems of many of the world's great conurbations are now subsidised by public subventions, yet when, as from time to time happens, a call is made for such transport to become self-supporting, how little attention is then paid to the resultant effect upon labour supply, upon firms' profitability, and hence on urban patterns! It is often said that employers in central London subsidise their employees' travel to work by means of higher wages (with the implication that this is 'uneconomic'). But such 'subsidies' are obviously rewarding, because it is there, in central London, that certain opportunities exist for creating wealth. It is in much the same way that subsidies to public housing in the central areas of cities can be rationalised: they ensure that the city as such keeps going, they at least attempt (whether perversely or not) to preserve its form, and in doing so they incidentally guarantee the prosperity of innumerable enterprises within it.

It is in America that the opposite perversion resulting from the fetish of quantification—the opposite, that is, to cost-benefit analysis—has found its fullest expression. There, everything seemingly has to 'pay'. (In some places, even the benches provided for your rest carry paying advertisements.) Hence, any new-town development undertaken in America (and there are a surprising number of these) is measured and judged by its financial success compared with that of normal small-scale speculative development. A faith in the profitability of 'community building' has none the less launched numerous such speculative ventures. Not surprisingly, perhaps, financial difficulties have hit a number of these ventures, and the credibility in America of new-town development as a tool of social policy has thereby been damaged.

The isolation, self-containment, conceived (even in America) as intrinsic to the notion of a 'new community' seems, in general, to have underlain many of these difficulties, as also have the problems of shouldering costs which in more 'normal' developments are publicly borne. At root, however, it is fallacious to think of a town (say) as a real-estate development. A town is more than the sum of its lots. This is true even if the public purse is bearing its due share of the facilities and amenities. It is that property already in a town—the old property, often written down —which gives new property there much of its value. The payment one makes for a house itself no more relates to—or in some sense 'truly' measures—that house alone than do cost-benefit calculations measure those things we do not pay for when we use them. The quotient of public housing in the British new towns is arguably far too high, but hopefully it does nevertheless simulate that presence of the poor and less well-off which gives to all expensive property some of its value. (A world in which everything was new would be unimaginable.) The American 'new community' developments have perforce concentrated upon houses for the affluent. That they have yet found themselves in financial difficulties should not be read as punishment for a failure of social responsibility, but rather as indication of how meaningless it can be in monetary terms to measure a form for which that measure never was devised—as also, how distorted that form will become if it must be bent to that scale which would measure it.

It is impossible to know, then, where to draw a categoric line between the subsidised and the profit-making activity. We all are parts one of another. The park may be free, the national art collection (in some countries) may charge an entrance fee, the railways may be run efficiently but at a loss—or even at a profit —and all such things will affect, in lesser or greater degree, those activities which institutionally are viable only if they make profits in the accounting sense. They will affect them, not least, through locational relationships: not, that is, through any direct involvement with those profit-making businesses as such, but through their mere proximity, such that they help determine the conditions under which those businesses operate. For, what can usefully be said is that the notion of a social environment is valid—as valid as that of a natural one; and that our understanding of such an environment, precisely because it is not concerned with those relationships which money mediates, does not very helpfully respond to financial measurements. And, of course, not only the 'subsidised' activities determine the environment of the profit-making ones: other profit-making activities, not financially connected one with another, must be conceived to do likewise. Here, perhaps, there may be the germ of an alternative approach to that which holds there is a measurable social truth and that financial units are what must define it.

In this respect, it can now perhaps be accepted that 'planning' —that is, land-use planning—is properly concerned with urban form and the forms of settlement generally. Further, the presumption can with increasing certainty be held, that if planning is at odds with economics this is not because the notion of form is unscientific and imprecise, but rather because planning as we now know it has been preoccupied with the preservation of certain stereotypes of forms no longer of relevance to life. It has not taken up its responsibility for guiding the emergence of forms that are new. Now, planning (as has been said) has to do with how A's affairs affect, say, X, Y, Z, who are not party to his affairs. It is concerned, in other words, not with some one measurable function or another, but with the social environment.

The idea of an environment, after all, is in a most fundamental way the concomitant of any idea that things exist in space— in our case, the space we call 'society'. A social body is an abstraction from social space, an abstraction which entails questions of choice, of selectivity, about action for that body. In any space so conceived, every selective action conveys consequences for bodies not concerned with that action yet occupying the same space. The sum of such consequences is the environment. (Pollution from a factory chimney—the very existence of the factory, standing where it is—affects the being of others in no way connected with its business. And this will be so, so long as that separate entity we know as 'a factory' remains for us a meaningful, separate form.) So long as 'society' continues to be something worth talking about, those bodies that busily function in it will do so in a social environment from which they cannot escape. That environment will not be measureable by those units serving to facilitate the functional needs of relationships between social bodies as such.

Of course, this conclusion is not easily swallowed by persons committed to revealing general laws that govern society by measuring all things social (whether or not money is paid for them) in common financial units. The pursuit of this course is what leads, in matters of policy, to social gigantism—the inclusion of all disparate activities in one great social calculus. The symptoms of this affliction are indeed prevalent around us in Britain today. Theoretically, then, one has to ask whether, after all, this is not possible: the elimination of the social environment as such. One can only answer that, in the virtually inconceivable circumstances of this being achieved, we should then no longer have cause to discourse about 'society': we should be speaking about Utopia. This, indeed, reveals in yet another way how our obsession with measurable social certainty is nothing but a last gasp of that fatal idealism which for so long has been the ruling philosophy of our culture.

To be free of subservience to measurement for its own sake, then, to be free of the passing fashion for cost-benefit analysis (which of its nature attempts to give a static validity to what life itself is often in process of discarding) is to be free to explore and, in so doing, to bring under the shelter of civilisation the new forms that are emerging. 'Planning' is concerned with the forms of the environment. The environment, indeed, has its forms, just as much as do the multiplicity of activities from which it is composed. The social environment is not merely the residue (as it were) of those activities. The conditions under which the latter take place, the elements common to so much that is disparate, can of course themselves be fashioned. We can make our towns pleasant and convenient if we wish—and if we care enough to want to do so. What we only need to remember, is that a town none the less remains but an environment (whether or not it 'pays' for itself is, by and large, irrelevant)—and that, being an environment, the many activities for which it is merely the setting retain their own importance, such that even if we moderate their functionings yet we cannot determine these. It is the bane of idealistic town-planning that, mistaking the town for the end in itself, it throttles the development of activities which must sometimes be allowed to change the very form of settlement.

the anatomy of city-regions

It seems, one must all too often destroy to create. It is necessary, as it has been here, to say what things are not in order to clear the ground for constructing what is. (The scale of our urban renewal problem, it might also be said, unfortunately but mirrors the mental renewal we yet must undertake.) But whereas one can destroy alone, it is much harder to create on one's own. To say effectively that the city no longer exists, then, is easier than to say what the city-region is. The city-region is only what the language-game we together play about it makes of it. I can at best, therefore, now only make certain propositions.

Obviously, the city-region is of its nature something widespread. This means more than that it is 'big'—though big it certainly is, as also, however, is a city. That it is 'widespread' says something about its structure. It indicates a certain kind of bigness: one moderated as to that inward concentration upon its own affairs typical of a city itself. The widespread character of the city-region, then, is obviously a reflection of its regional component—that component of some common factor which gives unity to an otherwise disparate area. The common factor of this region, in the terms we are now using, is seemingly the 'city'. Yet how is this possible, since the concept of the city is precisely of something which we think of as in itself contained and sufficient unto itself? This contradiction in terms—of the 'spread city'—can perhaps be resolved by acceptance of the proposition, that the dispersion of the city is being accompanied by the simultaneous disappearance, not just physically but from our minds, of that over against which the 'city' conventionally has acquired its character of isolation: namely, the 'countryside'. This is, indeed, the general situation in which we find it increasingly meaningful to discuss the city-region. Because 'rural' is losing its meaning—not least because 'rural' is often tantamount to fake—the city can spread.

It is helpful to think of the city-region as polycentric. This does not infer that a city itself has but one centre; indeed, we recognise that it has many. It infers, rather, that the many centres of the city-region have each an importance of their own and one that is not comparable each with the other. (There is no conceivable hierarchy for the centres of a city-region.) What this polycentric character of the city-region directly leads one to, however, is the dynamic quality of the city-region. For, if many centres of equal potential are conceived to exist in some related but non-hierarchical way, the connections between them are necessarily vital to the concept.

How, then, can something have significance as a centre, and yet be set in an environment in which not what it (the centre) is matters, but how it relates to that environment? In America, after all, prophets have for years been predicting the centre-less urban region. It must be admitted that in the more settled landscapes of Europe, or the eastern seaboard of America, the mere inertia of human geography provides centres, in the emergent city-regions there, such as in the California *tabula rasa* seem not to be necessary. Are not our ideas about centres, then, and about the 'communities' they are supposed to manifest, merely the residuals of folk-memory, comparable to the human appendix? Maybe so—and yet these appendices grumble away and, awhile, cannot be ignored.

Of what kind, however, are these centres of a polycentric region? To a certain point, they can still be considered all-purpose in character. They are such, in so far as the activities and functions of the old city-centre hive off indiscriminately into the surrounding region to build up the relative importance of the existing centres there—the commuter centres first: around London, your Guildfords, Maidenheads, Chelmsfords. Increasingly, however, the centres of a city-region tend to become functionally specialised. There are manufacturing centres like Slough, or the London new towns; office centres, like Croydon, or Ealing; and, of course, shopping centres in the now-established American fashion. Looking beyond the present to the emerging pattern, it does seem likely that the at present all-purpose centres themselves will become increasingly specialist in function. Perhaps the greatest example so far of this is in Holland, where The Hague, Amsterdam and Rotterdam are growing as parts of one great city-region—one, incidentally, that has been recognised as such and humanised—with a specialist base respectively in administration, industry and commerce, linked yet separate, with the city-region as a whole profiting from their mutual relationships.

There are sound enough reasons in principle for expecting this kind of specialist development to occur. The more spread becomes a city-region, the further apart from each other become its particular activities. The potential loss from this process evidently must be the greater for activities that are functionally related, than for those that are related only environmentally. A market of any kind, for instance—whether in vegetables or in stocks and shares—would of course stand to benefit from being in some neighbourhood where manifold other activities are carried on, where there are shops of all kinds, transport facilities, supplies of labour, etc. But its own cohesion as a market will be such as substantially to hold it together, to resist fragmentation, in face of any diffusion that its environment may suffer. (There will be, as it were, differential coefficients at work.) Such a market, itself subject to the diffusive influences of the city-region, can then well be imagined as constituting one of the dispersed, functionally-orientated centres of a growing city-region. (One thinks here of the new *Les Halles* of Paris.) Expressed in another way, the city-region might be conceived as a great complex of precincts.

This being perhaps granted, there yet remains the question of the dynamic of the city-region. Even if the city-region be polycentric, it is the setting in which these many centres find themselves that gives the concept its validity. And, of course, the dynamic is in the environment. This, in the crudest way, is expressed in the extraordinary criss-cross pattern of motorised travel that characterises any city-region. To the most unsophisticated eye, this is what immediately distinguishes the conurbation from the city-region. In the one, we have become inured to the tidal wave, morning and evening, of travel to work to and from the centre. In the other, one now witnesses the kaleidoscope of individual journeys, at traffic densities that do not vary greatly in any part of the region, moving in every possible direction throughout the twenty-four hours of the night and the day. In Detroit, for instance, work trips are now a lesser proportion of all journeys than shopping and other private trips, and are but a bare third of all kinds of auto journeys.

It is this idea of a dynamic environment that has to be grasped by anyone who would understand that the city-region is a new form of human settlement. This is an idea of social environment that is not of a merely passive backdrop to activities. The environment, if statically conceived, does perhaps lend support to the notion of the 'centre' as the quintessence of a settlement. Dynamically conceived, however, the environment makes more readily acceptable the polycentric character of the city-region.

The dynamism of the city-region is manifested in the physical mobility that one witnesses there. Underlying this mobility is a release of personal energies—really, of spiritual energy. Crudely as it often may be expressed—whether in the taking of a job merely for the money, or in the pretentiousness of the architecture of many dwellings (or, conversely, in the decent, unpretentious vernacular that we are now increasingly enjoying in some private speculative developments), or in the perhaps comically gregarious picnic habits of motorists—in all such ways, bonds about the ordinary person have yet been burst, to give him freedom unimaginable to his forebears; and the city-region is the manifestation of this outpouring of energy. This is no political manifestation—as, in the past, so many such outpourings have been and which we have become used to regarding as that manifestation proper to the radical human spirit. It is, rather, a new radicalism, one superseding politics (though John Kennedy recognised its political import), one that is restoring the idea of personality to the place of importance it has too long relinquished to the (hopeless) quests of social idealism.

To say all this is not to be saying that the city-region, because it exists, is right. The matter is more complex. There are, to be sure, forms of life we abhor; yet even these we might still be well advised to try to understand—rather than to suppose that by ignoring them we could kill them off. In the same way, we can allow that there may be 'good' forms, forms of which we find ourselves concerned to achieve fine examples, not just because for better or for worse we are stuck with them, but because in themselves they are the vehicles of our hopes or of our understandings. Of such have been the enduring forms of human settlement: cities, towns and villages. And, to these, if one believes that the full potential of humanity is yet being reached towards, should now be added (they, indeed, must to some extent be subtracted from it) the city-region. By the same token, of course, any example of such a form that falls short of our hopes, merits an abhorence all of its own.

There need be no pretence, indeed, that the life of a city-region is idyllic, that, because it is no longer as of the city, it must somehow be of a rural calm. Such life has its specific tensions—as also relaxations of tension—and the journeys of which so much of it is constituted are part of the human condition there. There is also, however, no question but that we have it in us to live on the level of tension the city-region demands of us. Those who move out to these areas do so precisely to be 'different'. Our sociologists, for sure, still fixed as they are upon the phenomena of the antique urban forms, have feared for a new human loneliness and (some of them) have banally attempted a pejorative diagnosis of 'new town blues'. In itself, this does not here merit space for refutation (others have painfully had to do this exercise). It is, however, perfectly true that the haphazard development of our metropolitan regions has led to personal suffering. The one-car family in a two-car situation; the car-less family where public transport cannot be justified (the hell of those few car-less ones in Los Angeles); the isolation of a minority of housewives; the superfluous travelling to work: all such examples might, hypothetically, be used to damn the total form of the city-region. To do so, however, would be hopelessly to underrate the forces that are producing that form. By the same token, however, it is not to deny those forces if we seek to order their effects differently. As for loneliness—that horror of the urban intellectual—whilst, arguably, it is a condition to which we are born and which we should not too easily allow life to disguise from us, it is something which the manifold benefits of life in a city-region do demonstrably sustain.

At all events, the forces leading families to locate themselves where each as a human cell hopes to find satisfaction, are proving strong enough to drag in their wake businesses in search of people to employ. Increasingly, firms are finding it profitable to locate themselves where their workers are to be found. The process is now reversed which once daily lured a tide of multitudes to the magnet of work. In so far as the work is moving to where the people are to be found, it is becoming dispersed and the tidal phenomenon dissipated. It was in 1963 that the commuter flow into central London first showed an absolute decline. Of especial interest, however, is the radical contribution made by the London new towns to the commuter problem of the city-region to which they have come to belong. These new towns are 'self-contained' only in a simplistic, static sense. That is, in very general terms (amongst them there are minor variations) they contain approximately as many jobs as people in employment. However, by no means everyone who works in any one of these towns also lives therein, and vice versa. Rather, the situation is a dynamic one. By 1961, for instance, those who travelled to work either into or out of Harlow were 36% of those who both lived and worked there. The figures for, say, Crawley and Welwyn (where there is an appreciable excess of jobs to residents in jobs) were 47·7% and 69·8% respectively. What puts these facts into perspective, however, is the comparison that can be made with the 'unplanned' parts of the growing London city-region. In Berkshire, for instance, between 1951 and 1966 journeys to work that crossed administrative boundaries increased at nearly four times the rate of local journeys within those boundaries. In the new towns, on the contrary—despite their yet far greater population growth—local journeys increased at 60% of the rate of journeys across boundaries. It only needs to be added that, again despite their phenomenal growth, the commuter flow from the new towns to central London itself has become an insignificant part of such commuting as they do generate. In 1966, for instance, the proportion of commuters from Stevenage to central London was 1·3% of residents in employment; from Harlow, 3·8%; from Basildon (the highest), 6·2%. Rather, the commuting phenomenon of the new towns is now strictly city-regional in character, concerned with journeys to and from other towns in their own vicinity. Here we can see foreshadowed, therefore, not only the way in which a city-region grows but the way and the agencies whereby that dynamic growth might be civilised.

Of course, businesses themselves need ever more space and, on that score alone, themselves have a motive to move. Indeed, all functions need more space. Urban areas, to provide at competitive standards for schools, for car-parks, for roads, for open spaces, etc., must veritably displace themselves. The high costs and the negligible gains of the high-rise, high-density solution to the problem of urban renewal are too well known to need repetition here. This is a solution that will, no doubt, continue to be sought so long as the tyrannies of our ideas about urban form manage, through political channels, to impose themselves upon those hapless ones too poor to escape such bigotries. Ultimately, however, urban areas can only displace themselves by a structural transformation—and this means, by taking upon themselves a city-regional form. If we wish still to live in a city, we shall have to seek that city across a region.

In all this scene of personal mobility, however, one fact stands out. The poor are never so mobile as are the better-off. This underscores the inescapable social problem, peculiar to the city-region and new to our times: the ghetto of the urban poor. In America, the urban poor are identified (and identify themselves) by colour, so that racialism is supposedly the great social problem there. But deeper than this, underlying the problem of race, is the problem of the urban poor. Europe will surely know it too. The outer London metropolitan region, for instance, is being populated overwhelmingly by people able to move out to it by buying their own houses therein, leaving behind them in central London a massive public-housing drive for the less well-off. Two social worlds are thus being created, perhaps more rapidly so than ever before.

One does not need much imagination to look ahead a few years and see those central wastelands of high municipal dwellings abandoned to all but the most indigent of our people. The fact has to be faced, that the mobilities of the city-region are socially segregative—and segregative in a more categoric way than anything we have hitherto known. The city-region enhances the technocratic tendencies of the present world. Those to whom its mobilities present the greatest opportunities it makes the more self-reliant, the less dependent upon their humbler fellows. Conversely, the old-fashioned city was a main generator of employment for the lower-income workers—the public transport workers, the caretakers, the shop assistants, traffic wardens, municipal workers generally. Such people, when jobs are extruded from that very city to which their employment is tied, at a rate rising more rapidly than that at which residence itself is moving, must find it the harder to be of use to an ever more technologically based economy. The bus driver, so necessary to keep a city functioning, when there is no longer a city to function, will not without some aid be able to contribute elsewhere to the new modes of life springing up. Incredibly, in Britain there are voices to be heard saying, in effect, that to preserve the poor we must preserve the city (it is sometimes phrased the other way round, but, in charity, this is what it can be taken to mean). It is indeed profoundly true that the poor contribute to our common civilisation. (It is, incidentally, equally true that many of the activities without which our civilisation would be inconceivable, in commerce as in industry, depend for their continuance upon the occupation of older properties, at lower rents. This is a fact of which the advocates of isolated new towns admittedly have taken too little account.) Yet it is, surely, a sour disposition that would advocate captivity of the poor, a permanent stamp upon them, in a place abandoned by their fellows. It reflects a mentality of despair, the syndrome of defeat. The city-region presents alternative possibilities to this, could we but bring ourselves to take them, possibilities that are the counterpart of its undoubted dangers—dangers because of which it is becoming urgent that there should be some public understanding of what form it is that nowadays we must treat.

These dangers are inescapable because city-regions are inescapable. And this is so because the satisfactions and rewards they proffer are so great. Life in a city-regional context is rich and is seen to be rich by great masses of people. In no respect is this more obvious than in that of recreation. Recreation takes place there against a green backcloth. Whether for the children, small or large, as grass and trees and water again become a part of their lives, or for the full family with ready access to open country and open skies, 'Nature' is not something apart and romantic that you find beyond the normal life of the city. It does not, indeed, require a great physical space to make this contact with Nature possible; it already begins, after all, when a playground is not of asphalt, but grass. Within the human scale, the refreshment provided by Nature yields rapidly increasing returns to its

---

7. The public impression that the London new towns had become commuter settlements must be held generally accountable for the discontinuance of that programme. What matters is not so much that the impression in question was essentially a myth, as that there has been a failure to grasp the very significant contribution being made by the new towns to the structuring of the London region. This contribution is illustrated by the 'independence indices' developed by Ray Thomas in his study, *Self-contained and balanced Communities*, for P.E.P. Of the index of commuting independence (ratio of local to crossing journeys) plotted against population size, Ray Thomas says: 'Most of the new towns stand out like trees from the summer undergrowth'. Yet this contribution to regional order happened by mistake. On the one hand, the region was not supposed to have developed as such, and thus has been regionally unplanned; on the other hand, being ideologically 'self-contained', the new towns, because they were not containing the growth of the 'city', were deemed to have been wrongly located. Ideology, therefore, has demanded remote new cities instead of new towns, and has left the city-region itself planless. The lesson, however, has now become plain: the proper place of new town development is indeed in the dynamic context of city-regions.

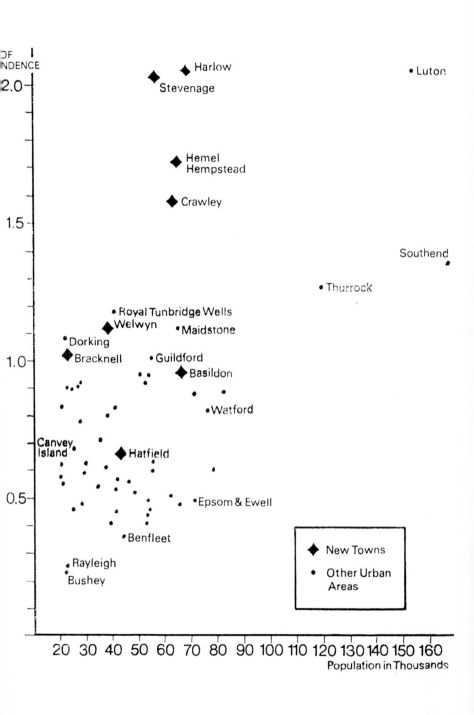

OF
NDENCE

2.0 ◆ Harlow
● Luton
◆ Stevenage

1.5

◆ Hemel
Hempstead

◆ Crawley

Southend

● Thurrock

● Royal Tunbridge Wells
◆ Welwyn
● Maidstone
● Dorking
◆ Bracknell
● Guildford
1.0
◆ Basildon

● Watford

Canvey
Island
◆ Hatfield

0.5
● Epsom & Ewell

● Benfleet

● Rayleigh
Bushey

	New Towns
◆	New Towns
●	Other Urban Areas

20 30 40 50 60 70 80 90 100 110 120 130 140 150 160
Population in Thousands

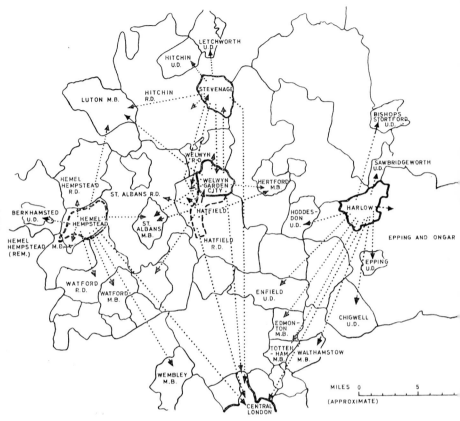

Areas to which 0.5 per cent or more New Town residents travelled to work in 1961

8. The commuter pattern of the London new towns is predominantly local. They have become centres within the region of great convenience to those concerned. They (and they alone) thus structure the region, not by being 'self-contained' but through the articulation they supply, such as gives a form upon which to base the planning of the region. From Hemel Hempstead, for instance, travel to central London in 1961 was only 9 per cent of its commuter traffic. Those who commuted from Hemel Hempstead formed 33·9 per cent of its employed population, and, to an overwhelming degree, they travelled locally. The overall picture is one of dynamic order.

(The map is taken from Audrey Ogilvy's pamphlet, *The Self-contained New Town*: Building Research Station, 1968.)

provision. Anyone who disparages the form of city-regional life because it is 'neither one thing nor another', because it is neither the crowded city nor the wilderness, himself speaks from some bigoted position removed from the lives of ordinary people. Of course, however, the haphazard development of our city-regions is rendering access to green spaces for recreation increasingly difficult. Because we have failed to recognise the form, we are not ordering it. Accordingly, we are all tripping over one another, each by his particular actions rendering the others' environment less enriching. The parks on a motor-car scale that the city-region must have if it is to become a civilised form are practically nowhere being provided.

Whether a city-region develops haphazardly or by planning, however, there is no disguising that it implies the end of many of our conventional ideas about 'community', and particularly of those ideas concerned with 'place'. This (essentially architectural) idea of 'place' is concerned with the fixing of personal identity, with 'finding oneself' through association with the abiding artifacts that human concourse creates. But neither human personality, nor community, are any longer—if they ever were—such uncomplicated entities as this notion would have us suppose. The structure of personality for anyone alive today mirrors the complexity of the city-region itself. We each simultaneously play many roles, have diverse interests—often with no other link between them than our own brittle selves. The problem of personal identification today, surely, centring as it does on the question of 'alienation', is that of finding the balance between these disparate parts and of sustaining the resultant tensions. It is not—if it ever was—that of total immersion in some world small enough somehow to be comprehensible in its entirety.

In just the same way, any inhabitant of a city-region belongs not to one but to many communities—communities of work, communities of travel and communities of leisure. Such communities may be miles apart from one another, or may have no locational significance; one of his communities may even be that of 'place' —to the limited extent, perhaps, that a weekly shopping expedition draws an inhabitant back always to the same locality for her (or his) shopping requirements. Whether the word 'community', however, any more has meaning if we seek to apply it to the city-region itself, is doubtful. The concept of community conveys, after all, something of a face-to-face relationship, but the circumstances are hard to imagine—they would conceivably occur through some chance meeting in a far-away land—in which a mutual acknowledgement of inhabiting one and the same city-region would establish an emotional bond between any two people. Precisely because, however, we have been in the habit of equating 'community' with those forms of settlement we hold valid—and we do this, surely, because our idealistic cast of thought induces us to seek forms that somehow enfold us totally—we should the more beware of not now granting the city-region the recognition it on its own grounds must have. The city-region is not a community, but rather an environment. As such, it profoundly revises our ideas even of the self.

To be more mundane for a moment, if one had to select one single factor to demonstrate the city-region's originality of form, one might well concentrate upon its ports. Not, of course, its sea-ports: rather, its airports. For, undoubtedly, this is where over the next few decades the phenomenal growth in shipments will occur and around which, as a result, great complexes of development will emerge. Here, moreover, the technological factors encouraging 'spread' operate with a vengeance. The requirements for air space to serve any one airport are such as to enforce separation of airports on the ground by great distances. These alone would be factors, even if there were no others, wrenching great cities apart. However, we still have not grasped this fact. We clutch still at grandiose schemes to keep alive what essentially is no more than the old concept of the muncipal airport. The whole sorry controversy over London's Third Airport, for instance, fundamentally has been nothing but a reluctance to face the changing nature of London itself. This has been so, right through from the initial absence of a London metropolitan regional plan—wherein those directly disadvantaged by this project could at least have seen how, by conformity to some recognisable order, it possibly might have made sense—to notions of some grandiose airport, in some remote locality, able to serve the whole of 'London'. These latter ideas are basically still in the railway age. They still conceive of a city with one centre to be served. On the contrary, air travel will turn the city inside out. Whereas the railways led, sector by sector, each to a terminal serving the whole city at its centre, the airports of city-regions must each serve a part of such regions but radiate therefrom in every direction. Not one gigantic airport, therefore, but a co-ordinated pattern of relatively smaller ones is what regional planning calls for in terms of the ports of the future. What mountains of difficulty we shall, however, make for ourselves if we do not recognise the forms that are taking shape around us! This, truly, is the road to barbarism.

The sociology of the city-region, then, has hardly begun to be mapped. (How could it be, when sociology has so strongly been posited upon the forms of the past?) Fortunately, there are now some admirable beginnings to this task. In the meantime, however, we must make do with sketches such as have occupied this chapter. It is not urgent, to be sure, that the city-region be sentimentalised. The term itself is hardly lovable; a desiccated air too much pervades it. Perhaps if we spoke of 'cloud cities', or of the 'open city', we should be more romantically attracted to the concept! What is urgent, rather, is that the idea should be understood—if only for our successors, because the environment man creates lasts a very long time, to refresh or stifle those who innocently inherit it. To be understood, things must be practised. Therefore, we must set about making our city-regions and fully accepting them—ceasing to pretend that really what we are doing is to extend the city, or to partake of the country, or that, anyway, someday we shall get back to these. It may even be that when the city-region comes thus to be understood it will also come to be loved—and then, perhaps, we shall find it a kindlier name.

. . . *so grows the tree*

The time then is past—if it ever was—for idealised representations of a world to be. It could of course be said, on behalf of such descriptions, that they are an aid to communication—that they open people's eyes as nothing else might to the unrecognised possibilities before them. Even if this were so, it were still better to eschew such an aid; the abuse suffered by Ebenezer Howard's consolidated schema is a sufficient warning of the misconceptions such a presentation is bound to engender. One doesn't want to risk a similar fate for the idea of the city-region. We would do better, rather, to stick to process, to how we would want things to happen. And if it be argued that one cannot discuss how things should happen without knowing what should happen, then it may be pointed out that our vision of the possible is tied to our conceptualisation of the actual. It is best to start as we do, therefore, from the strength of knowing something of what ordinary people's demands are of life today.

John Nash, in laying out Regent's Park as part of a city in a garden beyond the then great barrier of Oxford Street (a plan never fully realised), stands usefully as a simplified portent of present-day thinking. His visionary development there was posited on a recognition that, to persons having carriages, it would be of no great consequence should they find themselves a little apart from the busy centre of London's affairs. Accordingly, he set out to provide them with an environment that was neither town nor country—yet was, in terms of their actual circumstances, self-explanatory. Between Nash and ourselves, however, there is in practice one great gulf: not a difference ensuing from the advances of technology, but social in kind. Nash worked for clients for whom he sought actually to exploit the segregatory tendencies innate in the technology of communications. For us today, on the contrary, it would be intolerable and foolish to contemplate such exploitation. The reverse is the case. We in Britain have indeed but little time in which to prevent the social disaster of an emergence of ghettos of the urban poor. To recognise the city-region as a concept is, for us, as much as to resolve that somehow our common humanity must be expressed within it.

In speaking, as above, of 'we' and 'us', the intention is purposefully conveyed of a common interest in the civilising of the city-region. The optimism may seem forced. If so, it is only because the alternative does not bear contemplation. We must civilise this new environment, or culturally speaking we shall perish together. It is a cruel sidelight on the present urban tragedy in America that in those 'new communities' started by private developers there, and conveying the hopes of planners who rightly can see no solution to the problems of the cities within the cities themselves, to the residents of such developments 'planning' nevertheless precisely means exclusion of the poor. Planning in a sense, of course, this is: but bad, and possibly evil, planning. Planning in itself is no panacea. Nor is it even sufficient to announce that planning must recognise the new forms surrounding us. There is no neutrality possible for planning. The purpose of recognising the city-region is to make something of its society.

We are far even from recognising, however, the social shape that London is taking. Abercrombie in the 1940s proposed that, beyond the conurbation and the Green Belt, about five out of every six persons who settled in the metropolitan region should do so there in the planned developments of new towns. Whilst that theoretical picture of development has stayed before us, however, the reality has been precisely inverted. How amazing is our human power of self-deception! The society we actually live in has generated an outpouring of people into the metropolitan region such as is engulfing the unreal world for which we have planned. And the people in question are those who, under powerful personal impulsions, are buying their own houses and are demanding provision of land for those houses more forcibly than not only planners but government itself can contend with. It is, after all, an old, old story. Yet the irony of it, peculiar to our day and age, is that our planning ideology is denying any part whatsoever in this social evolution—in the society of regional London —to that sort of persons for whom, originally, planned developments had been chiefly intended.

The tragedy has been that new towns have, on ideological planning grounds, not been allowed to play their full social parts. Such a part as they have played, however, has been admirable. They have been the crucibles of our best hopes, places where a generation has found itself, and where the next generation is assuring our future. They have made a climate of opportunity wherein the unskilled have most readily become skilled. Against them, for sure, the criticism might be raised that they are predominantly artisan towns. This criticism would have some, but remarkably little, substance. Compared with London itself (not Great Britain), the new towns have quite average social residential compositions—through the spectrum, that is, from 'managers and professionals' to 'unskilled manual' workers. The details of this, though interesting, are not important here because they are insignificant in comparison with the inadequacy of the London new towns programme as such to assist with the housing of London's poor. It is not that there is a trivial imbalance in the social composition of the new towns themselves; it is that, because there are so few new towns, the ghettos are building up in London itself whilst the better-off naturally proliferate across the region.

We berate the Americans, because their concept of 'urban renewal' is one which clears away the slums in order to house the middle-classes—the slum-dwellers themselves being winnowed away to make new slums, God knows where else. We, under a more idealistic guise, are perpetrating the same disgrace. Of the unhappy options we give the urban poor in order to preserve our notions of the proper form of things, rather than a banishment to distant new cities the poor are naturally electing for tenement housing in the central areas—from which the other social classes are purchasing their escape. Not thus shall we avoid America's further experience of the disadvantaged urban poor: that which, in Detroit for example, now imposes upon negroes work trips 25% longer than for whites—and shopping trips 35% longer. We are ensuring that the same thing shall happen in Britain.

Currently, the housing drive in the area of the Greater London Council (the conurbation) is being stepped up from the 27,000 dwellings per annum at which it has been running (of which about 10,000 has been for private housing) to perhaps 45,000 dwellings per annum in the near future, with an anticipated fall in private dwellings. Demolitions are running at about 10,000 dwellings per annum, of which a component of clearance for new roadworks, etc. (rather than for obsolescence) accounts for perhaps 1,500. So that, given a total housing stock of about 2,500,000, the life-expectancy of a dwelling in the London conurbation is of the order of 250 years! In this festering sea of obsolescence, the poor will find themselves more and more alone. Even at this moment of writing, yet another in the sequence of haphazard governmental edicts has gone forth to make provision in the metropolitan region itself for a further 250,000 houses for private house-building; within seven years, in other words, almost another million of the better-off are to be provided with land, within an environment in all senses remote from that being provided for a similar number of the poor. John Nash, no doubt, would chuckle.

The inhibitions under which we act are extraordinary. Although our metropolitan regions, with their innumerable linkages, are the most fertile of grounds for economic growth, we draw back from cultivating that ground, from planning those regions as a means of realising the economic potential of which they are capable, because to do so would be to detract from our investment in the failure that our old industrial areas have unhappily become. We justify this resignation of responsibility upon the intuitive myth of 'congestion'—not bringing ourselves to face the analysis, deducible from simple geometry, that beyond the conurbation proper, in a London metropolitan region of, say, 4,500 square miles, we find a population density of the order of only two persons per acre. It is precisely here, in this kind of area, that firms should be allowed to seek their opportunities. Factories, offices, businesses, related by the mobilities at their command and prospering each from the vicinity of the others, in a great complex of enterprise, here out of enlightened self-interest might play their parts in fashioning a new form of life that awaits the touch of our understanding.

To provide both for prosperity and for communities that are socially balanced, then, what structure are we compelled to seek? It is not so much upon settlements themselves that, in answering this question, we should cast our eyes, but rather upon the great interstices between them. (The cement of a city-region is coloured green.) It is the distance between settlements that largely determines the size and character of those settlements. This is a question to which conventional physical planning can no longer debar access to economic considerations. There is a real cost involved in fostering projects at a remote distance from any supporting complex (as, in the interests of pristine apartness, physical planners have been wont to demand) and planners must be brought to account for the necessary financial inducements, regulative restrictions, and high discounted cash flows that such projects require if they are to become viable.

The question indeed can more reasonably be asked, not as to how far apart can we allow related settlements to be, but how close together might they not be? Have we not, in other words, more to learn from Los Angeles than Los Angeles from us? For, after all, Los Angeles is the archetypal city-region: it has grown up together with, not adapted itself to, the motor car. And it works. Whether you like it or not, it functions; it is not obscenely inefficient, as ordinary cities have become. Although the average journey to work there may currently have dropped by 5 m.p.h. from its target rate of 40 m.p.h., yet additional freeway construction will restore that position—and do so at a *per capita* cost (both capital and revenue) almost certainly lower than, say, for San Francisco's lauded new public-transport system. It is ominous, of course, that to achieve these results it becomes necessary for expenditure on freeways to increase at a somewhat higher rate than does population itself. Yet population increases phenomenally in Los Angeles—at about 2% per annum—because this is a great arena of opportunity for the ordinary person with mobility at his private command. Synonymously, it is the greatest agglomeration of single-family houses in the world; it has surpassed the housing standards that elsewhere are only dreamt about. For these reasons it is certainly true that we, isolated as in Europe we are in the haughty fortress of our minds, have more to learn from Los Angeles than it from us.

Yet, although certainly the realistic question for planners must henceforth be, 'Why not like Los Angeles?', none the less Los Angeles surely is not for imitation. There is, after all, the question of human 'roots', of personal identity. We do not all of us come—as do so many of the migrants to Los Angeles—from some imaginary Middle West. For sure, this concern of ours for 'roots' is perennial; it is inherent in man's nature—in that nature's inescapable divisions of itself—and it sometimes ensues in unreal and dangerously simplistic proposals. To recognise this question, therefore, is neither to predicate an ideal country, nor to reject as futile that concern about our 'roots'. Planning, then, has a responsibility if only tentatively to concern itself with the great contemporary issue of 'alienation', of the problem of personal identity, of the finding of oneself, which underlies all the sometimes violent questioning of the uncommitted young. To be strange to oneself, alienated, is a condition—however perhaps transient its pathology—to which the planning of our environment cannot be blind. In this light, Los Angeles to the rest of the world seems but intoxicated with its mobility. Indeed, perhaps for this very reason Los Angeles is to its credit questioning itself as no other place is doing; and as a result it seems to be seeking nodes of development within the great complex which constitutes it. Such a node, for instance, may prove to be the gigantic private development of the Irvine Ranch—90,000 acres, with a potential population, in a variety of townships, of at least 500,000. This development may hopefully prosper just because it has not been conceived—as so many romanticised American 'new communities' have been—as a barrier to the growth of a city, but rather as a structuring element of a city-region. What Los Angeles apparently needs, as much as do all our city-regions, is not that great flux it presently exhibits, but access for its inhabitants to such opportunity both of work and play as the self-respect of each person requires. That context, then, in which the person of today must find himself, his identity, might reasonably be expected to have elements of stability such as now are unknown to Los Angeles.

It is in any case our instinct—certainly in Britain—that between our settlements there should be areas of green. This deep, if uncalculated, feeling, until dislodged by considerations equally profound, we would surely be wise to abide by. It touches upon an instinct for contact with Nature and it is founded upon a common-sense recognition that areas must be shared in common if Nature is to be allowed to speak to us. The parks that in the past have made London (say) so civilised a city have hitherto expressed these feelings of ours. To secure adequate areas of green within the emergent city-region, however, how shall those pressures be resisted that would take what should remain open to us all into private use and enjoyment? For, if those areas be made too large—as, say, London's Expanded Green Belt would have made them—the forces creating the city-region, for lack of other outlets, will swamp their defences and compromise their value. We have, therefore, to conceive of models achieving tolerable balances between the forces that would join and those that would keep apart the parts of any city-region. (What we cannot suppose is that distances might separate those parts such that effectively no forces would occur between them.) We have, for instance, to judge as wisely as we may the level of commuting between settlements such as would not make untenable the spaces we want to preserve between them. We have, therefore, to consider the balance between job opportunity and mobility of the home, between the turnover of jobs and of residences. We have to do this, furthermore, within the context of the differential mobility of social classes and income levels. The different level of availability of job alternatives to different income levels will be a significant parameter determining the size of such separate urban developments (and hence of job availability therein) as we might plan for if we wish to limit the temptations of commuting out of those communities. Furthermore, this needs to be considered in terms of the job-promotion spiral and its attendant age-structure. (Indeed, might it not be our purpose to make of our city-regions places away from which people, as they now do, in old age do not retire?) In all this, then, the planning of the city-region can perhaps helpfully be thought of—if physical analogies are indeed helpful—in terms of entropy, of a dynamic state of order in that environment of which it consists.

Several years after the concept of the city-region began in painful discourse to be formulated amongst planners, 'research' in Britain—at least as far as the role of new towns in the London city-region is concerned—is beginning to articulate the form. The precision this brings is much to be welcomed. These illustrations of an idea, moreover—the idea, that is, of a dynamic urban order—being sanctified as 'research', they may well give courage to policy makers to discard their old casts of thought and accept new ones. We shall soon be possessed of much clearer ideas of how the size of settlements in a city-region, their distances apart, the character of their growth—either as comprehensively developed, or as permissively generated entities—how these factors bear upon job opportunities, social composition, patterns of travel, home circumstances, and so forth. Research, however, even be it pursued to the end of time, will not tell us what action is right or wrong. What, nevertheless, it already seems certain to do, is to suggest that if the city-region is a form about which we should discourse, then the establishment of new towns therein, as key agents of its structure, is the main clue to the civilising of that form. 'Civilising', because that balance each epoch must seek, in the light of its particular circumstances, between association and dissociation—the distances apart men would keep from one another, and the society they would make together—the articulation of the forms by which they in a human sense exist, all this is what the new town in a regional context serves to achieve. If this be so, how great a tragedy has been the rejection of the new town —because of its supposed failure of idealistic 'self-containment'— as an instrument of city-regional development! New towns are precisely the process whereby city-regions should be fashioned.

In any case, however, research will not suggest ideal solutions to the planning of our city-regions. Concerned as we must be with process, we must in each case proceed with the geography that is already there. Also, just as we must acknowledge variety in our future environments, so we must accept that mistakes will be made. From the wide range of existing patterns of development, as many different solutions again may come. For the Paris region, for instance, they have chosen to develop in a broad corridor towards Rouen, creating a tangential axis to oppose the normal radial development. (Have they not, one wonders, over-emphasised the force of the radial effect in a city-region?) For the Washington region (and others), a star-shaped pattern, accepting the radials but ordering them, has been agreed. The discussion attending each such decision is compelling, if never conclusive. Indeed, it remains very much to be seen whether the patterns will be fulfilled. What matters, rather, is that in these cases the city-regional form has been recognised and is being articulated. It is preferable to chaos.

It is not, in any case, with the making of patterns that we should be concerned. Our problems are immediate ones and to help solve them we have our immediate experience. If we could now accept—and this would be the radical change—that it is in our metropolitan regions themselves (and not either beyond them, nor, alone, in the old city cores) that our planning problems exist to be solved, we should therefore properly be dictated to by the possibilities those regions extend. We must accept that those regions should be structured by developing their existing communities comprehensively and by developing new towns within them. We know that the social balance in those communities must, in order to dissolve the inner ghettos, be somewhat changed. We do not know for sure whether the post-war new towns, had they but allowed for a normal ratio of private development to public (as, in future, new towns must do) and had they taken their full share of the really poor, would have generated more than the relatively little commuting they have done, nor whether they might wisely have aimed at different population targets—but we are within sight of intelligent reconsiderations about all this. What is certain, is that there should have been many more of such projects. In the Paris region, again, they have settled for 'new towns' of the order of 400,000. In Britain, in discussing metropolitan regional new towns we are coming to think rather in terms closer to 100,000. The discussion, again, is in each case reasonably persuasive, but never conclusive. There is room in any city-region for a great range of settlements— and not least, by any means, room for villages. In the London region places like Guildford, Maidenhead, Bishops Stortford, Chelmsford, Tunbridge Wells, Bracknell (where an office centre more important than Croydon should have been stimulated), Crawley, Aylesbury and many others wait to play their roles as the nodal points of a new order. And the Green Belt, of course, awaits the reformulation of a more rational open-space policy. Nor is there any hierarchy to be imposed. Instead there is flux. Mobility is the stamp of the city-region—mobility that is ordered, and therefore pleasant and creative, not least because it occurs between localities that enjoy their own measure of stability. This, then, is a form that owns no final definition and the creation of which is itself an experiment.

There are various other relevant things that we do know, helpful to the continuing process of planning a city-region. Colin Buchanan has suggested, for instance, that at normal British town densities we cannot hope to provide 'full motorisation' in communities—assuming some modern layout planning—much above the order of 100,000. And 'full motorisation' is something the denial of which planners will increasingly have to account for. Again, we know that a satellite community like, say, Yate, about eight miles from Bristol, remains a commuters' town and, at great cost to the majority of its inhabitants, therefore merely extends its parent city in the most inconvenient way possible. On the other hand, the London new towns, about twelve miles from the conurbation and twenty from the city centre, have with their present socio-economic composition both mastered their central London commuter problem and amply proved their attractiveness to employment. Again, with more remote projects like Bletchley or the new Milton Keynes—say, fifty miles from the

city centre—the doubts and the difficulties of development pre-
dominate. A city-regional planner's imaginary manual or hand-
book, therefore, might well lead him by and large to phase the
development of settlements of the order of 100,000 at distances
from one another of about a dozen miles.

Of course, however, if such a planner were ever tempted to
blanket his city-region with some such grid of communities, he
would in no time find local circumstances that destroyed his
pattern. Prominent among these would be the tendency, pre-
viously noted, of the parts of a city-region towards specialisation.
The internal and external relationships of a manufacturing and
of a commercial community will not be conducive to identical
growth or targets, nor will those of, say, a general manufacturing
town *vis-à-vis* those of a specialist one, the demand for whose
particular product may (and often should be allowed to) run away
with any planning preconceptions about its desirable size.

Now, there is an admitted element of expediency in this
general approach to city-regional planning. The expediency here
in mind, however, is very different from that which inadvertently
has dominated planning action in Britain in the recent past. In
this latter case, the establishment of remote new cities, as also of
minor projects under the Town Development Act, has been at the
mercy of local politics. Planners with their 'overspill' have only
been able to go where they were asked—and the motives for
these invitations have sometimes been doubtfully conducive to
the success of the projects. This has meant that the developments
in question could not be supportive one of another; the development of Swindon, say, lends nothing to the development of
Milton Keynes. The isolation from which the projects evolving
from official planning policy anyway suffer, is thus aggravated by
this surrender to political expediency.

Of course, however, this raises another and very real question
—for local politics are not a factor that planners can ignore. Indeed, the planning of the city-region runs immediately into the
realities of local politics. The best illustration of this is the saga of
Milton Keynes itself. Fortuitously in 1964, to the aid of a government seeking to implement *The South East Study's* strategy of

new cities, there came the home county of Buckinghamshire. Bucks, of its own initiative, proposed a new city of 250,000—to be built upon the then fashionable linear plan—in the north of the county and therein as remote from London as possible. After much discussion (and the abandonment of linearity) this has become the officially approved new city of Milton Keynes. Is it too far-fetched to suppose that this initiative on the part of the elders of Bucks was due to a desire to keep 'London' at bay and away from their pleasant front garden? And would it not be in order to point out that they are in fact going to end up, most messily, both with Milton Keynes and with London? This is, indeed, the crux. The city-region as a new social form indeed imposes painful political reconsiderations; it is, however, not to be toyed with. Without courage, politics could not anyway long be conducted. Mere guile does not of itself long sustain those who are party to it. A major political prize, therefore, awaits whosoever is first to recognise the latent power of our city-regions as a form of life attractive to great masses of our people.

Through all this theme of flux and controlled expediency, however, there is one constant: the 'green'. In the situations we envisage, recreational access to natural things—that luxury now in principle available to all, of a green setting to their lives—is a *sine qua non*. Parks must on an almost unrecognisable scale become the formative agents of our new city-regions. Without them, we will not civilise what we anyway shall do. And there will, of course, be ample space for these parks, in the interstices between the communities we envisage. Perhaps the first task a planner of the London region should set himself would be to identify, in or near the Green Belt, say ten new parks, each of 10,000 acres. Landscape architecture on the grandest scale must have a recrudescence in this parkland. (We shall not, however, need to have recourse to Nash's tricks of 'apparent space'.) The vulgar jibe about the 'broiler-house civilisation' of our metropolitan regions is in any case a banality, but it also conveys an ignorant fear about the living-space at our command. This uncomprehending fear has its counterpart, interestingly enough, in a well-meaning governmental policy of sponsoring 'country parks' but of doing so, not in city-regions where they would succeed, but in that imaginary void between cities, the so-called 'countryside' itself. In the regions of tomorrow, rather, golf courses will constitute our city squares.

Whether agriculture, however, could continue to play a serious part in these areas of green is a question that must honestly be faced. Experience in America shows that various intensive and relatively physically insulated forms of farming continue to thrive within city-regions—even in those quite disorderly ones typical of America. The difficulties of conventional farming in proximity to highly populated areas, however, are a commonplace amongst farmers. Some drop in yields, some less intensive system—e.g. grazing—may have to be accepted. This point should not be exaggerated, however, not only because proximity to markets—e.g. for greencrops and for dairying—would provide agriculture with some material compensations, but because the normal annual increase in agricultural productivity is providing, in Britain, so great a margin of compensation—approximately, to the power of 10—for our losses of agricultural land. There is one special point, however, about agricultural land in city-regions and this is, that such land is already and in very high degree serving an amenity purpose. Part-time farmers, the nearer one gets to any large conurbation, own an extraordinarily high percentage of the land. The point is not that these farmers are not reasonably productive—there is no justification, by and large, for this accusation—but that they own the land primarily for the pleasure it gives them and are fortunate enough to be able to capitalise it quite intensively. The amenity value of such land, therefore, foreshadows the structure of land-use in a city-region planned humanely to accord—as, for example, the Paris plan has done—the topmost of priorities to areas for people's leisure. The more, therefore, the city-region is constructively developed—and this is what agricultural interests should seize upon—the less becomes the threat to full-time farmers of arbitrary deprivation of their land for remote new cities.

It is when people realise—as, by now, any reader surely must have done—that any discourse about city-regions requires of them to accept that within each of our present metropolitan areas many millions more might be accommodated, to conduct therein precisely the kind of lives they would wish to conduct . . . it is then that it commonly breaks in upon people that we are dealing in terms of a new form. The change overtaking us is a traumatic one. From this point, then, one is free to emphasise the growing irrelevance of the old built-up city centre. This centre conceptually becomes not a meeting-point but merely an obstruction to mobility, like a mountain or a river barrier. Indeed, should we ever become seriously alarmed at the prospect of some city-region acquiring too wide a spread, there would be no stronger device for binding this region together again than by constructing trans-urban motorways across it, to connect the outer parts thereof one to another, but allowing thereon no access or exit within the old, irrelevant conurbation. We are, perhaps, some way from actively considering a proposal of this kind, which yet may appear somewhat futuristic, but in so far as we accept the new form of the city-region, there is no limit to the irrelevance, as a separate entity, of the old conurbation.

What cannot be avoided, however, is some practical view of the future of our old conurbations in the light of the possibilities of metropolitan region development. If we indeed allow ourselves to think in the new way about the capacity of our metropolitan areas, it follows that we shall be able to accept the obsolescence of the conurbations for the miserable fact that it is. Our inability now to face this fact, and the physical decay that ensues therefrom, largely stems from our difficulty in accepting that urban form has changed. This is what, above all, is responsible for the short-sighted remedy, which will surely be ever more widely canvassed, of patching up enormous areas of decaying houses such as, on social and economic grounds, any nation without a beam in its eye would recognise should be demolished.

The beam in question is, of course, the relocation of people in such numbers—sometimes whole neighbourhoods—now called for by the state of obsolescence into which Britain's housing stock has fallen, so that politicians understandably cannot face the social implications. We can see here, cruelly exposed, the twisted relationship between housing and planning and how the one does not statistically and neatly fit to the other; how, indeed, housing *or* planning is becoming the truer syndrome. We in Britain are demolishing slums now, unbelievably, at a lower rate—far lower, despite the greater size of the problem—even than before the last war. In the 1960s, such demolition has been of the order of 60,000 slums per annum; in the late 1930s, it was of the order of 90,000 per annum. It is hardly surprising, therefore, that now we should, in cold statistics about something foul, find ourselves staring at the true order of our obsolescence. What we have not yet brought ourselves to look full in the face, however, is the programme of demolition into which we should enter. Merely to keep pace with current obsolescence we should be pulling down houses at the rate of at least 150,000 per annum. To catch up with our shameful backlog, the figure to which this rate should be raised is, of course, a matter for argument. But we now know fairly objectively there are one-and-a-half million houses (out of a total stock of about fifteen million) actually unfit to live in at this moment. To clear them in ten years, say, would raise the demolition rate by 150,000 to 300,000 per annum. Disguise this fact from ourselves as we may, this none the less is the measure of our economic and social degeneration.

Disguise it, indeed, we are trying to do—as is normal with anything too painful to face. A policy of patching up the nation's decaying housing stock is being eagerly embraced by politicians. Economically, as with all poor men's strategems, such a policy is disastrously short-sighted. Socially, however, it commends itself to politicians because, hopefully, it would cushion the impact of the sheer size of the relocation problem which our negligence has allowed to develop. In so doing, nevertheless, it would delay the restructuring of our urban forms and imprison a further generation in social obsolescence.

It is, surely, because our minds have been cast in the old moulds about urban form that really we have not seen any alternative to allowing our housing thus to fester where it is. It is, for sure, then, only to the regions around our cities—and of which those cities now have become but a part—that we can with any hope look for deliverance from these problems. Rather than to remote new cities, it is to these city-regions we must look for the rehousing of those displaced by slum clearance. In our hearts we all of us now also know that the building of more tenement slabs within the conurbation is too great a human price to pay for the architectural gratification which originally motivated such a policy. All that is left, therefore, is a planning policy focused upon the city-region.

There is, of course, a case for the patching-up of housing. As a rule-of-thumb, for instance, an informed consensus about the economic life of an average house might put this at about 80 years. (Local Authorities must amortise public housing over only 60 years—and no one should deceive themselves that preservation of a house much beyond that time is somehow a forced saving of capital.) During the latter part of its economic life, however, capital improvements (or 'patching up') will certainly be worth making to a house. This policy, then, is applicable to those six million houses in Britain which, as we now know, are not actually unfit to live in but are deficient of basic amenities. There should be no illusions, however, about the cost of this sort of exercise. If this cost is faced up to—and we cannot afford not to face up to it—the irony of a 'patching up' housing policy would be that it would create middle-class areas at the expense of the poorer classes. After all, this is what the renovation of Canonbury in London has done—and it is anybody's guess how many working-class families a Canonbury or a Chelsea displaces in favour of middle-class immigrants: a ratio of 3 to 1 might be a reasonable surmise. Now, there is nothing inherently wrong in this. Indeed, it is very important for the whole civilisation of a city-region that a middle-class element should be attracted back into the older areas—and, even, that subsidies to achieve this should be entertained. In proportion as this is done, however, simultaneously a far greater provision must be made elsewhere in the city-region for the less well-off people displaced by this process. To restore planning and housing to a harmony, therefore, will be a complex business. In so doing, however, we must be guided by the principle that the city-region is not the city and its region, but a thing in itself, whose regional character permeates the whole of it and in which the social classes are not to be segregated into separate parts.

It still remains true that a static and predetermined representation of the ideal city-region is to be avoided. One cannot say to just what lesser densities the old conurbation should be redeveloped. What certainly must be resisted is the reactionary notion that, as large central areas come up for redevelopment—say, like Covent Garden—they each must be treated as citadels of quintessential urbanity. Precincts, rather, are to what such areas commend themselves in the context of regional form. What surely must happen, however, is that, if the dynamic of the city-region be harnessed, the re-creation of the old will proceed in phase with the new. If those urban poor in need of rehousing have options allowing them to move within that region to which by all manner of threads they are attached, the clearance of areas of obsolescent housing will be so much the more facilitated and hastened. This, in turn, will condition our ideas of the densities at which, from time to time, to redevelop the central areas.

Indeed it is this dynamic element, when all is said and done, which ultimately distinguishes the concept of the city-region from our older planning forms. It is this, likewise, that must bring tumbling down the planner's omniscience—tied to ideal solutions as this has been—and simultaneously brings back into his field of vision those ordinary people whose personal enterprise and resources are anyway making it inescapable for him, the planner, to discourse about city-regions. These people of enterprise have, under the old dispensation of ideas, all too often found themselves at odds with the planners. It may be too that our planners, because the emergence of city-regions is at last forcing them to admit social and economic considerations into their thinking, will themselves come to seem more human in the process. In forgoing the satisfactions of delineating plans for a perfect world, at ever more meaningless distances in time, planners may be compensated by participating in the everyday excitements of actually causing things to happen. The dynamics of the city-region will thus change our concept of planning and our very notion of what it is to make a plan.

Should all this happen it will be because, instead of involving ourselves in the contradictions inseparable from forms that no longer are relevant to life, our actions—those of planners and people alike—will be directed in terms of a form that is meaningful. In an imperfect world in which folly and injustice are no doubt endemic, and perhaps nothing really changes, the articulation of new forms provides the best excuse for our perseverance with humanity as an agent of change—as also, ultimately, for any discourse between ourselves at all. If we recognise this, we shall have returned to that concern for a realisation of the potential of the ordinary human being, from which, an Age ago, Ebenezer Howard started his crusade.

an idiosyncratic bibliography

Colin Clark, *Population Growth and Land Use*: Macmillan, London, 1967. By an economist who realistically accepts the dynamic of social development.

Robert Dickenson, *The City Region in Western Europe*: Routledge, London, 1967. A helpful text-book.

Edward Eichler and Marshall Caplan, *The Community Builders*: University of California Press, 1967. A disillusioned account of American 'new community' experience, not to be ignored for its challenging practicality, but posited on the dubious criterion of 'profitability'.

Erik H. Erikson, *Insight and Responsibility*: W. W. Norton & Co., New York, 1964. Erikson is attempting the exploration of that vital territory between psychiatry and sociology, between the person and social structure.

C. B. Fawcett, *The Provinces of England*: Hutchinson Home University Library, London, 1960. The classic (1919) polemic of British regionalism, now again in fashion.

Donald L. Foley, *Controlling London's Growth*: University of California Press, 1963. A sympathetic but incredulous look at the ruling doctrines of British planning.

Herbert J. Gans, *The Levittowners*: Allen Lane, The Penguin Press, London, 1967. This book establishes, with reverberating consequences, that suburbanites are also people—contrary to the dominant supposition of the intelligentsia.

Peter Hall, *The World Cities*: Weidenfeld and Nicolson, London, 1966. An indispensable review of the world-wide phenomenon of the urban revolution.

Ebenezer Howard, *Garden Cities of Tomorrow*: Faber & Faber, London, 1898. The seminal book of British—as arguably, of world—planning.

Jane Jacobs, *The Death and Life of Great American Cities*: Random House and Jonathan Cape, 1962. Urban romanticism at its best—or worst. The stranded intellectual virulently laments the disintegrating city; all planning reduced to the scale of Greenwich Village.

F. J. Osborn, *Green-Belt Cities*: Evelyn, Adams & Mackay, London, 1969. By Howard's great disciple, who has been responsible for a measure of realisation of his ideas; an embodiment of practical humanity.

P. Self, *Cities in Flood*: Faber & Faber, London, 1957. A formative work in the emergence of the new structure of planning concepts.

Derek Senior, ed., *The Regional City*: Longmans, London, 1966. Affords a look into that painful process of discourse (here, an Anglo-American colloquy) whereby new concepts are hammered out.

Ray Thomas, *Self-contained and Balanced Communities*: P.E.P., London, 1969. The London new towns are revealed in some depth in their proper role, as structuring agents of a dynamic region.

Raymond Vernon, *The Myth and Reality of our Urban Problems*: Harvard University Press, 1966. A quietly authoratitive demolition of the pretensions of the upholders of 'urbanity'.

Peter Winch, *The Idea of a Social Science*: Routledge, London, 1958. Draws the inferences of Wittgenstein's thought for the study of society, which thereby it will be found to have set on a different course.

M. Young and P. Willmott, *Family and Kinship in East London*: Routledge, London, 1957. Its honesty of bias has been less scrupulously noted by partisans of the urban status quo.

In Britain during the past few years a significant proportion of the formative literature on planning has been contained in reports commissioned by the Government. The anomalous position in which the government has thus found itself is a cause for reflection. At root, however, this trend constitutes a comment on the failure of the normal sources of ideas—confined as these have been within conventional structures of thought—to contribute to the practical management of a radically changing situation. Alas, the official voice has itself, with but a sophisticated veneer, too much served merely to articulate conventional thinking.

The following official reports are amongst the most significant:

Northampton, Bedford and North Bucks Study: H.M.S.O., 1965. Wilson and Womersley's report on the feasibility of a new city for London overspill—but chiefly used as a vehicle of exposition for the idea of the 'linear city'.

The South East Study: H.M.S.O., 1964. Perhaps the last of the 'classical' plans.

The South Hampshire Study: H.M.S.O., 1966. An encouraging example (by Buchanan and associates) of maturing professionalism in regional planning, imaginative and socially realistic—but still ahead of political acceptability.

Traffic in Towns (The Buchanan Report): H.M.S.O., 1963. An attempt to reconcile city and automobile—yet lacking the sociological and economic analysis which would have moderated the enthusiasm it first generated.